". . . understands the importance of preparing the actual work process and begins the book with an in-depth analysis of the trust and the systemic considerations necessary for success. The book does not simply provide generic instructions and then leave you out to dry. [It] works on the premise that a virtual team can have the cohesiveness to equal, if not surpass, existing productivity levels present in a person-to-person office."—**Colorado Woman News**

"How are you going to guide, coach, and evaluate your team when you lay eyes on them just four times a year? Take a look at *Working Virtually*."—"Ask Annie" column, **Fortune Magazine**

"Managers involved first hand with off-site employees will find Hoefling's advice and checklists most useful."—**Publishers Weekly**

"A practical guide to help organizations prepare people, systems, and structures for a smooth transition or expansion into a virtual environment . . . [including] telecommuting, virtual conferencing, e-learning, and other applications. Her book includes information on how to develop a virtual work environment and how to build and manage virtual teams."—**Denver Business Journal**

"The book has a huge number of practical tips and tools. It provides many tables and lists that will be extraordinarily helpful to anyone responsible for implementing or managing a team. *Working Virtually* is an invaluable resource for the law firm assessing virtual effectiveness, and for any firm wanting to support virtual teams."—**Law Practice Management**

"This is a tremendous book. It is substantive, well-researched, conceptually sound, and practical, all at the same time. If you want *the* handbook for building, implementing, and sustaining virtual teams and work groups, buy this book."—**William E. Schneider**, Corporate Development Group, Inc., and author of *The Reengineering Alternative*

"Trina Hoefling's insights, recommendations, and easily implementable nuts-and-bolts checklists will help transform the most entrenched bricks-and-mortar organization into a telecommuting-ready enterprise. *Working Virtually* lets us all see just how do-able, productive, and rewarding the virtual work environment can be."—**Jennifer J. Johnson**, Founder and Chief Virtualist, Johnson & Company, The Virtual Agency™

"This is both a very practical and comprehensive guide to the factors that contribute to effective virtual teams. It offers a solid primer in the collaborative tools currently available. The great utility of this book is its pragmatic, cookbook approach to putting the human and organizational structures in place that will enable a virtual team to succeed; and in explaining why these structures are important."—**Carol Willett,** Executive VP for Learning and Innovation, Applied Knowledge Group, Inc. (www.akgroup.com)

"*Working Virtually* brings the growing world of 'distributed work' into a strategic perspective. Trina Hoefling not only highlights the important distinctions between virtual workgroups and virtual *teams*, but also provides detailed practical steps and tools for implementation and management. It provides a bridge across the chasm. This is a book the CEO should read first . . . then pass along to all key managers."—**David P. Mead,** President and CEO, TSI Services, Inc., a Telecommuting Consulting and Training Services firm

"An enlightening book! Trina Hoefling has helped me better understand how we can effectively and efficiently work virtually. She has a gift of communicating in a compelling and practical manner that inspires one to action. This is a must read book for anyone considering a virtual work environment."—**Robert A. Garcia,** Director, International Truck and Engine University

WORKING VIRTUALLY

WORKING VIRTUALLY

Managing People for Successful Virtual Teams and Organizations

Trina Hoefling

STERLING, VIRGINIA

First Published in 2001 by

Stylus Publishing, LLC
22883 Quicksilver Drive
Sterling, Virginia 20166

Published in paperback 2003

Library of Congress Cataloging-in-Publication-Data

Hoefling, Trina, 1958–
    Working virtually : managing people for successful virtual teams and organizations / Trina Hoefling.—1st ed.
       p.   cm.
    Includes bibliographical references.
    ISBN 1-57922-032-0 (alk. paper)
    ISBN (paperback) 1-57922-069-X (alk. paper)
    1. Virtual reality in management.   2. Teams in the workplace—Computer networks.   3. Organizational effectiveness.   4. Personal management. I. Title.
    HD30.2122 .H63   2001
    658.3—dc21   2001020091

First edition, 2001
ISBN: hardcover 1-57922-032-0
Paperback reprint, 2003
ISBN: paperback 1-57922-069-X

Printed in the United States of America

Printed on acid free paper

For those who believe, who care, who struggle, who have learned to not struggle. For those with the courage to commit to whatever brings more light to the world.

CONTENTS

SECTION TWO:
IMPLEMENTING VIRTUAL TEAMS

SECTION THREE: MANAGING VIRTUALITY

SECTION FOUR:
ORGANIZATIONALLY DISPERSED

and Collective • The Magic Word Is . . . "Network" • Knowledge
Management for Dummies

ACKNOWLEDGMENTS

This book has been percolating for a long time. A twinkle in my eye. A couple editors and publishing houses believed in it enough to encourage me, and John at Stylus Publishing convinced me to move forward. That was the easy part. Then it had to be developed and birthed. I am blessed with angelic midwives, to whom I am eternally grateful.

Thank you, Kara, Toni P, Moriah, and Marianne, my abiding earth angels who always believed in me, this book, and who never saw this process as anything but valuable and complete.

I cannot begin to name so many other earth and spirit angels. Some of you know who you are, and some have no idea how your energy, spirit, belief, and love have helped me to hold the space for the transformation occurring within me, my work, the world and this book.

I'd also like to thank

- Dave Mead for believing so fully in virtual work, and for pulling together such strong and competent teams over the years.

- My fellow RBA'ers and the Virtual Hot Tubbers.

- Clients, colleagues, virtual dialoguers, past customers and so, so many blessed and valued friends and members of my heart and soul family.

INTRODUCTION
THE VIRTUAL WORKFORCE OF THE (NOW) FUTURE

It's not so much that we're afraid of change or so in love with the old ways, but it's that place in between that we fear . . . It's like being between trapezes. It's Linus when his blanket is in the dryer. There's nothing to hold on to.
                                                              —Marilyn Ferguson

There is no lostness like that which comes to a man [sic] when a perfect and certain pattern has dissolved about him.
                                                              —John Steinbeck

Peter Drucker tells the story of the first management conference called in 1882 by the German Post Office. The topic—and only CEO's were invited—was how not to be afraid of the telephone. Nobody showed up. The invitees were insulted. The idea that they should use telephones was unthinkable. The telephone was for underlings.

The same story could have been told ten years ago about executives and the personal computer. Now no one is without at least one. Not many years ago virtual work was a "novel idea" employed to retain that exceptional employee with life circumstances that required flexibility, or a management fad that others were doing that would surely fail due to lack of management controls. Many companies still are unclear how to "control" virtual employees—or even if they can or should—and worry that to become increasingly virtual requires a major strategic change rather than incremental improvements in current operations.

Today companies must go outside brick and mortar corporate walls to recruit and retain the best talent and profitable partnerships. A global marketplace demands global companies. Customers demand products and service support that is adaptive, flexible, and integrated. Independent and project-specific contractors are a fundamental part of the workforce. Cross-organizational strategic alliances are common-place. In a tight labor market, employees demand more choice and flex-ibility. Real estate costs prohibit boundless expansion. These market drivers have invited organizations—perhaps yours—to explore virtual work.

Enabling technology has made virtual work practical. Collabora-tive software and expanded bandwidth have changed the way we think not only of basic work processes, but also the way organizations them-selves are built and managed. We have the technological capability to work across time and distance. Work moves to the people rather than people moving to the work. Virtual teams and virtual work have and will continue to shift our thinking about how companies function today. Remote work is not new or unusual anymore, but, for most, it is not yet familiar ground. Is it a strategic breakthrough or an incre-mental improvement? That all depends. . . .

Many organizations are reluctantly embracing virtual work; it is a growing reality for a number of pragmatic foot draggers. Virtual work is easily viable, yet human nature remains the key to success. The key to satisfaction and success for a virtual worker is a real sense of con-nection to fellow team members and their organizations.

Why This Book Now, Who It's for and What It Accomplishes

If you are leading or part of an organization that is implementing or considering implementation of virtual work—telecommuting, virtual teams, global expansion—then this book is a critical tool to help you prepare people, systems, and structures for a smooth transition or expansion into a virtual environment.

I developed one of the first remote management training programs in 1984, before telecommuting and virtual work had a name, in an effort to address the need of engineers who were leading matrix-based project teams built on expertise, not geography. I have since worked with many individuals and organizations to implement virtual work strategies. This book summarizes the wisdom, learnings, and client experiences gleaned from almost two decades of work in the field.

This book is both practical at a team implementation level and organizationwide. It looks at the impact that distributed work has on organizations' systems, structures, leadership, and cultures. It examines the bottom line impact for organizations that shift their way of thinking about knowledge management, leadership, mentoring, business processes, and workflow. Human resource professionals, managers, CEOs, information officers, knowledge managers, as well as team leaders and members will benefit from the systemic perspective provided. Written for the organizational member, the reader does not need to be an organization development expert to find value.

This book examines and develops the guidelines for creating infrastructures and tools that will enable you successfully to support the human element of distributed teams, enabling people to collaborate effectively across distances and differences. It goes beyond tips and tools, however, by asking—and answering—the following questions:

"How does the organization achieve its strategic priorities by developing itself into an increasingly virtual environment?"

By taking a systemic organizational approach, exploring knowledge management and learning organization principles, and applying them to a virtual environment, this book gives you the practical guidance you need as a leader or team member to develop your organization into a high performance, broad-based, decision-making federation of geographically dispersed and committed organization members who support and feel supported by their organizations. Section One focuses on developing answers to these questions through sharing learnings and practices of pioneer organizations that have created a supportive environment for virtual work and virtual teams.

"How does working virtually work?"

The solid advice and proven tools which are captured in Sections Two and Three will enable team members and leaders, human resource professionals, and organizations to develop and manage high-functioning virtual work teams whose team members find a sense of connection to work and the team.

"Can virtual organizations be learning organizations?"

Section Four expands on the importance of knowledge management and emerging leadership mentoring models in an increasingly virtual work world. It also looks at the probable future of networked organizations.

Basic guidelines and tools are provided for the team leader or virtual member who needs to form, develop, and facilitate productive and functional virtual teams. The team leader, manager, or human resources professional will find invaluable assistance in developing support for virtual team managers and members. One can pick up the book and go directly to the chapters that provide practical instruction for those charged with virtual team development and find the nuts and bolts assistance needed to get started or troubleshoot virtual team issues effectively.

Are We Crossing the Chasm?

Visionaries Versus Pragmatists

Many business leaders today are in a quandary. By nature, most organizations are conservative. The leadership waits to try "new things" until others have clearly proven that something is a "good buy." Geoffrey Moore, in *Crossing the Chasm*,[1] discusses the early market for innovative technology products and the mainstream market of people who want the benefits of new technology but who do not want to have to "fuss with or fix it."

Virtual work seems to have an adoption cycle that is similar to the way business adopts technological innovations. Innovators and early adopters have been practicing elements of virtual work for years. Innovators aggressively pursued the opportunity to implement technical tools to enable distributed work simply because they were intrigued by the possibilities. Early adopters may not have been as technologically

---

[1]Geoffrey A. Moore, *Crossing the Chasm* (New York: HarperCollins Publishers, 1991).

intrigued, but they saw the potential and were willing to implement virtual work based on their own intuition and vision.

The trick is in crossing the chasm from the visionaries and adventurers to the pragmatists, who are the majority of business decision makers today. They wait out passing fads, want to see well-established references, and ideally wait for some kind of established standard. The good news is that virtual work has been tried, works, and does not need to be piloted repeatedly. The bad news, which this book remedies, is that the successes and templates have not been well documented, nor has the impact on organizations' structures and systems been well defined.

Virtual work is a process for moving work through an organization, as well as a way of being aligned around a business mission. The majority contingency is skeptical; crossing the chasm requires expanding virtual work based on proven, established critical success factors that will integrate into the existing organization with little to no negative impact. The pragmatic majority wants it to "work." How well it will work for your organization depends on how aligned your processes, systems, and group identity behaviors are with a virtual work environment. This book helps the pragmatic majority assess the ease with which virtual work will integrate into their organizations, and provides practical tools and guidelines for how to get started or expand.

The Need—and the Readiness—Is Here

Distributed work is here to stay. Of the Fortune 1000 companies, 950 have formally implemented virtual work, often in the form of telecommuting. Of 31,000 companies over 1000 employees, 52 percent have formal virtual work programs. Known names such as General Electric, IBM, American Express, Hewlett Packard, International Truck & Engine, Xerox, the United States Government, and Nortel Networks are all committed to virtual work, so it's not just for the telephony and high tech industry anymore. Call center managers a few short years ago would not consider remote agents; today call centers are frequently expanding without walls by utilizing the capabilities of the Automatic Call Distributor and its remote management capabilities. Distance and online learning are no longer progressive and expensive technologies reserved for the few; virtual universities are commonplace and expected. People are realizing it can be done, and the technology is becoming more transparent.

Obviously, technology is the largest enabler of successful virtual work solutions. Both synchronous and asynchronous collaborative tools make virtual work not only viable, but also practical. For innovators and early adopters, this is enough. For the pragmatic majority, however, the market usually drives trends.

Three major market drivers have caused virtual work to increase exponentially:

1. *Real Estate Savings.* Companies are growing and real estate is expensive, so if a company can disperse its employees, having them co-located in less geographically expensive places and/or in people's homes, there's a tremendous savings that falls directly to the bottom line.

2. *Productivity Gains.* The major stated barrier to virtual work by managers continues to be, "How do we know remote employees are really working?" When productivity is actually measured, however, companies find that productivity increases significantly. Companies' self-reported productivity increases range typically from 15 to 48 percent in a virtual work environment. Call center agents are 5 to 17 percent more productive than their in-center counterparts. Professional support staff productivity gains average from 20 to 80 percent. The early findings suggest that the higher the skill level of the knowledge worker, the greater the productivity gain. What companies realized they were really doing was empowering people to work in the environment that is most conducive to any particular activity. For example, if a task requires thinking time, one wants a quiet, removed environment where distractions are reduced or eliminated. That is seldom a traditional office environment.

3. *Recruitment and Retention.* This has turned out to be a most significant market driver. Quality of life, work/life balance, and flexibility are increasingly important to people. According to a recent Conference Board Survey, 25 percent of employees would

change jobs if they could work from home, even if nothing else in their pay or benefits improved. There is currently a labor shortage in almost every job category and profession. No organization wants to lose its best people because of a long commute or a spouse relocation or because somebody wants to be available for the kids after school. Virtual work flexibility has become one of the top recruitment tools available today.

Transformational Concepts: Vital Mind Shifts That Make Virtual Work Succeed

How one *thinks* defines what one sees, expects, creates. How we think organizationally about work place, work relationships, and collaboration may be the single largest indicator of organizational success in an increasingly virtual world.

Mind Shift #1: Not Really New, But a True Paradigm Shift to Virtual as Viable

If your company is outsourcing, telecommuting, or dispersed geographically, you are a virtual organization. Distributed work is not really new, but to think of organizations as virtual is a true paradigm shift. We need new mental models, competencies, and practices. This is a change for most organizations. It changes how companies and leaders think of themselves. "Integration" and "collaboration" are more than just technological capabilities. Companies themselves must come to define themselves as collaborative, organic systems with integrated structures built on relationship, not hierarchy. It is easy to connect technically and create common platforms; it is quite another matter to think of the organization as fully integrated with itself, its vendors, its customers—as an open system with fluid boundaries. Virtual work changes the way the organization defines itself, work, and management.

While virtual work geographically allows greater distances and crosses multiple time zones, it also relies more on relationships and alliances forged by electronic handshakes. Trust is being reintroduced into teams as a fundamental principle. Power is placed in relationships and networks, not hierarchy or functional silos. Communication lines are broader and more open than any traditional multifloored high rise with chains of command and "elevators" of succession.

A flexible technologically connected and cross-collaborative organization is the vision, and the vision is more likely to be achieved with virtual work. Unfortunately, not enough virtual team development is being done to ensure that work is productive and satisfying in cyberspace.

Organizations have the opportunity to:

- Transform a virtual workforce into a functioning virtual organization with viable virtual teams who find meaning and satisfaction from the work and the team—across time and distance.

- Collaboratively join together within and among asynchronous and geographically disbursed organizations and people, and address systemic issues and opportunities.

It may seem counterintuitive to link as or more cohesively across time and space than happens typically in person, but it is only counterintuitive from the old paradigm and belief system of command and control, tribes and silos, and centralization/decentralization.

Another growing reality in organizations today is that of team members belonging to multiple teams simultaneously—based on function, project, customer, community of practice, task forces, and so on. Traditionally, employees were core members of one "fixed" team, usually a department, with occasional committees or task forces in addition to their core "jobs." Today, more employees are shifting team memberships or holding multiple, simultaneous team memberships, and their identification with a team also shifts accordingly.

There are many types of virtual teams. In today's global marketplace, most executive teams are virtual already, comprised of leaders across the organization based on their position and responsibilities, not place. These teams are ongoing leaders for the organization and usually have some face-to-face and much virtual collaboration.

A growing virtual team category is communities of practice based on interest or profession. The focus is usually on shared experience and shared learning, and membership is often voluntary. Professional trade groups are examples of communities of practice. As organizations align and cross strategic boundaries, and sometimes within organizations themselves, communities of practice are growing. For example, special interest groups are formed internally within organizations, such as people of color, gender, or sexual orientation. These groups are available only to members of the organization who fit any additional criteria, and they have charters and goals of their own. More and more, virtuality is a way to link these communities together across locations.

Project teams and task forces are mission- or task-specific. Members are usually members of multiple teams simultaneously and are selected for various reasons, such as expertise, representation, career path, or interest. Project teams can be short term or ongoing for the life of a project. Ongoing work groups are often functionally, customer-hubbed, or process driven based on value streams. Many work team virtual members are telecommuters or field employees (road warriors).

Teams are also increasingly comprised of members that cross organizational boundaries, including customers, strategic partners, vendors, and others. Some teams are ongoing, and some change or end based on need. For example, one well-known highly decentralized company maintains a huge knowledge management infrastructure, placing extreme value on information. Most of their teams have auxiliary members that are included in information loops. Senior management is kept involved as well as cross-functional experts and other stakeholders. These auxiliary team members are not part of the core production team, but they are virtually built into the team feedback loops.

Team members commonly may also be members of an established team, while joining a new team just formulating, and possibly joining a third team that is already formed but adding or replacing members. Teams form and re-form readily. The proverbial revolving door is the entry and exit for some team members. An Internet-distributed joke states that you know you are an employee in the 90s when you've worked for five organizations in two years without changing desks. The joke is more real than not. Added to this complexity, teams often answer to more than one "customer" or "boss," often share team leadership, and are virtual. All this serves to increase team leaders' and organizational leaders' need to build their capacities for leading and managing virtual teams across time, space, and organizational boundaries.

This book describes how to reframe the perception of your organization into one that is truly global, distributed, and virtual, and that aligns with the nature of how teams function today.

Mind Shift # 2: A New Blueprint of Organizational Environments Built on Electronic Networks

The *American Heritage Dictionary* defines "virtual" as "existing or resulting in essence or effect though not in actual fact, form, or name." Virtual reality suggests a simulation that is so lifelike as to feel real, but is not, in fact, real. "Virtual teaming" and "virtual work" can take on that same feeling of "essential closeness, but not realness." They are catchy phrases, but they may be misnamed. For organizations to successfully integrate virtual work, it needs to be redefined. It is not a "close approximation" of work, but a viable alternative way of working. Distributed work exists. It is real. It is sustainable. It is not second best based on circumstances. And it is not compromise, mirage, or simulation. It is not an overlay, replication, or poor substitute. Leaders and organizations need to begin thinking of virtual work as distributed work, not a compromised situation.

Increasingly, organizations are challenged by employees, contractors, and clients to redefine work as a process of relationship building among a host of stakeholders, both inside and outside the formal walls of the organization. By using teams and virtual work as a way of organizing the workplace, a new sociology is being born. Communities are creating and building on the Internet daily. The number of host sites for virtual communities on any interest to instant message, chat, schedule, and store knowledge and communication streams expands daily. Many of us open our email each day to several virtual community messages from people we talk to frequently but have never met. Romantic matches are made, friendships deepen in cyberspace, knowledge is shared among strangers based on a simple request for help—all prove that the old-fashioned handshake networking strategy is alive and well in cyberspace today.

The electronic handshake moves people into connection. How much more powerful can the collaboration be in a work team that is committed to a compelling purpose and vision?

Yet, in most companies today the overriding perception continues to be that a virtual team is a poor substitute for co-located work based on unfortunate circumstances. Many managers charged with implementing virtual teams attempt to have the group meet in person as much as possible and then replicate or "make do" with inferior communication strategies in between "real meetings." Group dynamics, ground rules, and meeting guidelines are rolled over to a virtual environment with little regard to the effectiveness of the fit. Not every dynamic, rule, or guideline needs to change in a virtual environment, nor should they. *Yet some should.* With collaborative software, huge opportunities to actually enhance group process are being missed because of people's tendency to stick with the tried and familiar.

The capabilities of technology change the way we think not only of basic work processes, but also of the way organizations and teams are built and managed. DSL, broadband cable, Web TV, PBX Extenders, intranets and extranets, VPNs, integrated supply chains, online communities, smart cards and smart devices, wireless devices integrated with the Internet—all expand what is possible.

It's the way people think about the concepts of teaming and meeting and communicating that is the bigger challenge. Work is becoming people-centric, not place-centric. Networks are the workplace, not a building. It is no longer necessary to go to a PLACE to perform basic functions—buy, sell, perform work, perform research, share information, and communicate. Virtual work can draw talent quickly from different functions, locations, and organizations. The goal is to leverage intellectual capital and apply it as quickly as possible. It gives organizations the agility to increase speed, expand expertise, and access strategic alliances to better meet customer demands.

Organizations can distribute organizational learning faster through knowledge sharing networks of functional, professional, or customer-hubbed "communities." Jarvenpaa and Leidner write that ". . . you cannot build network organizations on electronic networks alone . . . we will probably need an entirely new sociology of organizations."[2] Further, Grenier and Metes state that "Networking is not an adjunct to the work at hand; it is the basic virtual work process."[3]

---

[2]Sirkka L. Jarvenpaa and Dorothy E. Leidner, "Communication and Trust in Global Virtual Teams" (*Journal of Computer-Mediated Communication* 3(4), June 1998).
[3]Ray Grenier and George Metes, *Going Virtual: Moving Your Organization into the 21st Century* (Englewood Cliffs, NJ: Prentice Hall, 1995).

Networks—human and electronic—have traditionally been valued as vehicles or tools leading to a specific result, such as resource finding or a communication vehicle. It becomes fundamentally more powerful to think of networking as the process itself—how work gets done, teams get built, knowledge gets shared, and complexity gets managed. The organization of the near future is literally and figuratively built around the interconnectivity of virtual, human, and electronic networks, not the workplace per se.

This book will enable you to make the essential shift in thinking to understand the network as the workplace rather than the geographical location(s), which in turn will expand your concept of the organization itself, its marketplace limitations and opportunities, and talent pool options.

Mind Shift #3: Commitment and Engagement beyond "Doing My Job"

Since the industrial age, organizational leaders and management consultants have been trying to re-create a sense of camaraderie through engaging employees' commitment and connection to more than their job description. Without pursuing the effectiveness of these efforts, it is relevant to say that in an increasingly virtual work world, organization members are more geographically and physically isolated not only from their team members, but from their organizations, and sometimes their customers. At the same time, many people desire and require a greater sense of meaning and purpose from their work, and seek belonging to something greater than themselves.

On a practical level, if distributed team members do not have a clear sense of commitment, connection, and how their work "fits in" with the overall plan, individual efforts run a greater risk of being misaligned with the strategic priorities and organizational mission. Virtual work demands individual and organizational commitment beyond a job description to ensure connection, purpose, meaning, and right focus. The commitment has to come not just from the work itself, but in the way the group finds and interacts and depends on itself and each other. Individually and collectively, the "virtual job" is about outputs and relationship management, about process and a way of working.

Organizations, employees, even contractors increasingly seek connection to the workplace community as part of their identity. How do companies meet customer needs and motivate employees to commit to that mission? Instead of motivating people to merely "show up" at work and "produce," managers are seeking ways to motivate people to also apply their intellect and creativity. Clear communication and workplace community building is increasingly regarded as a critical component of each individual's job description, role, and responsibility. Books, consultants, and leaders cry in the wilderness about operating the organization from a systemic and networking point of view, rather than a mechanical and bureaucratic one. Virtual work forces the issue; networking is not an option.

Many workers today are knowledge workers, not producers on a mechanical assembly line. Labor's contribution is primarily mental, not muscle. These same employees and contractors are expecting to have a voice in defining the quality of their work lives and organizations, a self-definition that goes beyond being merely "resources" to use or discard at will. Cross-functional teams are expected to practice boundary crossing. In order for this collection of individuals to begin functioning as a community, the barriers are—or need to be—falling between managers and employees, between teams and teams, and between bureaucracies and serving the customers.

What makes an organization an entity that takes on a consciousness, a "life" of its own? It is a collective of the thinking and feeling that is held in common by its members, a "creation of some jointly imagined possibility."[4] It is not, as is commonly believed, an entity that preexists and to which people merely contribute "outputs," but an organism ever changing based on the collective beliefs of its members, hopefully all focused together on aligning with mission, vision, and goals.

Whether co-located or distributed, organization members are more committed to the organization when they see how they contribute to its very existence. This is hard enough to do in a co-located workplace. The virtual environment appears to run the risk of increased disconnection and isolation, *and it may* if the organization's leaders do not

---

[4]John Niremberg, *The Living Organization* (Burr Ridge, IL: Irving Professional Publishing, 1993).

shift toward a more holistic, systemic view of individual members' relationships to the collective "whole." The community—the collective itself—takes on power, precedence, and focus, rather than the rugged corporate machine which utilizes people and financial resources to achieve goals. This connection to the workplace community is based on communication, networks, and relationships.

In a virtual environment, the obvious barriers to community and connection disappear or, at least, become less visible—barriers like status, office size and other perks, unconscious cultural biases, communication across organizational levels. With virtual work, communication and relationship building are not only skills, but also a responsibility to "push" information out to the system and relevant individuals, as well as "pull" knowledge from the system when needed. No longer is the training department solely responsible for employees' training and development; individuals themselves are expected to seek out what they need.

Workplace community building has been viewed by most as an organizational ideal, but it doesn't need to be only a utopian future. If the interaction among people is the actual process of work, it is the promise of virtual teams to redefine interaction, which makes boundary crossing and network development truly powerful. Virtual teams are part of larger virtual organizations and are deeply embedded within the larger whole. Rather than creating more distance, virtual teams make increased connection possible by using relationship rather than geography as the connecting point.

This book provides guidelines for how to create the systems, infrastructures, and processes to support relationship connection through distributed communities rather than functional limitations. Electronic networking tools and groupware can bypass the silos and systemically support full access by all to organizational membership that is a higher-level membership than merely functional responsibility.

Mind Shift #4: Systemic Alignment for Collaboration, Interdependency, and Open Learning

Part of creating this emerging community-based organization is to encourage a collegial mindset among organizational members, a willingness to share knowledge and experience openly and actively, rather than defining one's value by how much knowledge and expertise one holds. Knowledge management/sharing is the newest, hottest field and is intricately linked with successful virtual work environments. Tacit knowledge has traditionally been shared accidentally or surreptitiously by the few to the few, and is often based on proximity, functional mentoring, and personal liking. In the emerging and boundary-crossing global marketplace, and with the interactive database and "smart" technology capabilities, the organization obviously benefits from encouraging organizational members to give forth their knowledge rather than hold back.

This concept, however, fundamentally changes the culture of most organizations. Traditionally, individuals are rewarded based on their rugged individualism built on their proprietary wealth of knowledge, resources, and contacts. If a networked community mentality is to emerge, organizational learning and knowledge sharing incentives must preside. Hoarding information as power can be a cultural barrier to full success of virtual work. In a virtual work environment, a robust knowledge management/sharing infrastructure and culturally aligned incentives are the best ways to quickly enable team members to access information and resources they need. Just as today one individual can access, through a focused search and a mouse click, a universe of knowledge on the World Wide Web, so can a virtual team member access a wealth of organizational knowledge without leaving the computer terminal. Likewise, training is no longer reserved for a "learning event." While classrooms and other synchronous training opportunities still have value, so does the need for continuous and readily available node learning on a just-in-time basis. Synchronous and asynchronous learning mechanisms support virtual team members' need to access support when and how they need it.

This book defines clearly how to realign your organization in order to fully support viable virtual work, and what technology and software, minimally, is needed to create a collaborative environment.

SECTION ONE

DEVELOPING A SUSTAINABLE VIRTUAL WORK ENVIRONMENT

Whatever you can do, or dream you can, begin it. Boldness has genius, power, and magic in it.

—Goethe

We have modified our environment so radically that we must modify ourselves in order to exist in this new environment.

—Norbert Wiener

I

SETTING THE INTENTION
AND DEFINING SOME TERMS

"Would you tell me, please, which way I ought to walk from here?"
"That depends a good deal on where you want to get to," said the Cat.
"I don't much care where," said Alice.
"Then it doesn't matter which way you go," said the Cat.
                    —Lewis *Carroll's* Alice's Adventures in Wonderland

Clarifying the Intention and Defining Some Terms

This book will use certain terms and phrases freely. Words become common, but don't carry the same meaning for everyone. To ensure common understanding, let's clarify what the difference is between a work group and a team, and what the intentions are for each. A few other terms have also become part of our business vocabulary, but, for the sake of clarity and shared meaning, will be defined again here in this chapter.

Work Groups Versus Teams
There is often a misperception of what is a team. Many work groups call themselves teams, but they're not. The first question a team leader has to ask is, "Is this really a team, or is this a work group?" Not all

work groups have to become teams. Hens in a hen house are co-located and are all expected to perform the same task—lay eggs. Their charter of laying eggs, however, does not require them to work together to accomplish that task. In fact, to charter a hen house with cooperation for laying eggs wouldn't make much sense and would probably, in fact, slow down production.

There are four basic criteria that a work group must meet before they can truly be considered a team, despite what popular definitions of team abound. Do you manage a "work group" or a "team"?

1. *The group must have some charter for working together.* Is there a shared purpose or shared mission and a shared vision? Are team members co-responsible for whatever the product or the service or the outcome is that they're there to do? A symphony, for example, is chartered with creating and performing beautiful, harmonious music.

2. *The group must be interdependent.* Individual musicians in a symphony cannot perform the same music without one another's contributions. Working together is essential to achieve their charter. The product is truly team-created. The team members must be committed to working together as a group to achieve their charter. If a violinist in a symphony wants to strike out on a solo career, she can do that, but she will no longer be part of the team/symphony, unless an ongoing commitment is there to continue as a symphony member as well.

3. *The team must be committed to working together.* If the group is reticent to work together for any reason, some commitment making becomes a first priority. The previously mentioned violinist may be a virtuoso performer, but if her commitment lies with a solo career to exclusion, then it is probably not in the best interest of the symphony to insist on her continuing membership with them.

4. *The team must be accountable as a unit to someone or something in the larger organization.* A mistake many organizations make is to reward and compensate people individually while expecting team cooperation. In keeping with the symphony metaphor, if the

musicians are paid individually based on demonstrating their superior musical skills, even if it interferes with harmonious sound, there is less incentive for the musicians to work together. Vying for solos and standout performances are more likely if it leads to bonuses based on individual virtuosity.

If these four criteria are not in place, you can have a virtual work group, but people will work autonomously and independently from one another. They may or may not be doing the same work. It doesn't really matter.

To become a virtual team in more than name only, team members have to find synergies and communication methodologies. Advances in technologies and groupware make this increasingly possible. In many ways, a virtual team is just like any other team, only more so. Just like in any team, you don't have to be best friends, but there needs to be some reasonable rapport, respect, and confidence in one another's competency.

Not all virtual work groups have to—or should—become teams, but it does impact how the virtual work groups are managed and function. There are a few obvious advantages to this, as well as some not so obvious disadvantages. Before exploring the cautions, let's first ask if a work group should function as a group or a team, and whether that determination should change in a virtual work environment. As far as should it change in a virtual environment, the answer is "No." The first question, however, prompts a series of other questions that managers and team members can ask before making a decision about team or work group, such as the following:

- Can more than one person cooperating together do the work better?

- Are the members naturally interdependent? How interdependent?

- Can results and/or evaluation be group driven?

- Is the final output a combination of group and individual contributions? Even in true teams, the answer is often yes. This is well suited for virtual teaming. If the output is exclusively group interaction, only virtual team members who are exceedingly competent with virtual collaboration will do well in a continuously virtual and collaborative environment. Fortunately, most work is a combination of group and individual contributions. Often, teaming is a combination of virtual and co-located environments.

If teaming is appropriate, but your team does not meet the four criteria, a first task is to meet the criteria before and as you move the team into a virtual environment. Later chapters provide tips and tools for developing work groups into virtual teams. If teaming is not necessary, a virtual work group is possible, but without some of the complexities of interdependence, commitment to one another, and group accountability.

Aha, so the trick is to create virtual work groups, not teams, right? Well, maybe, but consider a few points carefully before making the decision. Virtual team managers' temptation is often to hire independent folks and set up a virtual work group that does not need to interact with each other much if at all. Employees report and deliver primarily through the manager, and produce individually regardless of other virtual members' production. This hen house philosophy can be good, but if virtual team members are too independent, it may interfere with a team orientation when desired, and it may interfere with the members' sense of belonging, satisfaction, and commitment to the organization.

Virtual teams cannot be any more cohesive than a traditional, co-located team; therefore, it is important to lay a good foundation first. Commitment and satisfaction are critical to stay connected with virtual team members and the organization. Research conducted for the Society of Human Resource Management Foundation[5] uncovered some important facts regarding teamwork and the importance of interdependence.

These findings should be considered carefully before deciding whether to strive for virtual work groups or virtual teams.

A team's degree of task interdependence (degree to which team members must rely on each other to accomplish a work product) correlates with the degree of team members' organizational commitment.

---

[5]James Wallace Bishop and K. Dora Scott, *HRM Magazine*, SHRM Foundation Research, February 1997.

This challenges a virtual manager's natural tendency to decrease the amount of collaboration and cooperation required by distributed work group members. If high commitment to the organization is desired, a teaming environment is preferred.

If a virtual manager seeks to manage a group of individuals, complete task autonomy is appropriate. The research found, however, that a team's degree of task interdependence correlates with the degree of members' team commitment. The more interaction and interdependence which naturally occurs among team members, the greater their commitment is to each other and to the team. In virtual work, then, the infrastructure should support frequent and ongoing interaction, collaboration, and cooperation.

A team's degree of task interdependence also correlates with individual members' willingness to help each other. The more team members have to rely on one another, the more likely and willing they are to do so. Again, the network is the emerging workplace, and interdependence supports networks and networking.

Basic Terms

Collaboration: *Merriam-Webster's Collegiate Dictionary* defines collaboration as, "Working jointly with others or together, especially in an intellectual endeavor." It has also come to mean working with any of several electronic tools within an intranet, extranet, or the Internet.

Community: Community typically refers to a geographic area or social group based on interest (e.g., online communities of interest or professional communities of practice). The word "community" has old roots, going back to the Indo-European base *mei,* meaning "change" or "exchange." Apparently this joined with another root, *kom,* meaning "with," to produce an Indo-European word kommein: shared by all. The idea of "change or exchange, shared by all," is pretty close to the sense of community in organizations today. Community building is a core strategy for sharing among all its members the burdens and the benefits of change and exchange. As organizations become more networked, global, and virtual, "community" takes on even more importance.[6]

---

[6]Peter Senge, et al., *The Fifth Discipline Fieldbook: Strategies and Tools for Building a Learning Organization* (New York: Doubleday, 1994).

Intimacy: The word "intimacy" stems from the Latin "intimatus," to make something known to someone else. (Another derivation is the verb "intimate," which originally meant "to notify.") In its original meaning, in other words, intimacy did not mean emotional closeness, but the willingness to pass on honest information. This is the essence of knowledge sharing in organizations.[7]

Learning Organization: A learning organization is one in which people at all levels, individually and collectively, are continually increasing their capacity to produce results that matter. Chris Argyris and Don Schone describe organizational learning as questioning and rebuilding existing perspectives, interpretation frameworks, and decision premises.

Learning: Two Chinese characters represent the word "learning." The first character means to study. It is composed of two parts: a symbol that means, "to accumulate knowledge," above a symbol for a child in a doorway. The second character means to practice constantly, and it shows a bird developing the ability to leave the nest. The upper symbol represents flying, the lower symbol, youth. "Study" and "practice constantly," together, suggest that learning should mean: "mastery of the way of self-improvement."[8]

In a learning organization, learning is participation in a community, not an exclusively individual pursuit. The sustainability of a robust network community rests on opportunities for learning that leverage knowledge through collaboration. This is even more critical in a virtual work world.

Knowledge Management/Sharing: KM is a distributed hypermedia system for managing knowledge in organizations. It goes beyond the storage and manipulation of information. The goal is to find ways that support the transformation of individuals' personal knowledge into organizational knowledge by recognizing what is in people's brains and converting it to an organization asset that can be accessed and used by others.

Knowledge management covers three main knowledge activities: generation, codification, and transfer through processing knowledge

---

[7]Senge, et al., *The Fifth Discipline Fieldbook.*
[8]Senge, et al., *The Fifth Discipline Fieldbook.*

(how to); cataloguing knowledge (what is); and capturing historical, experiential knowledge (what was).[9]

Network: Again, four formal definitions come from *Merriam-Webster's Collegiate Dictionary*:

1. a fabric or structure of cords or wires that cross at regular intervals and are knotted or secured at the crossings

2. an interconnected or interrelated chain, group, or system (e.g., a network of hotels)

3. a system of computers, terminals, and databases connected by communications lines

4. to join (as computers) in a network.

For the purposes of this book, a network may mean all of the above. Primarily, it is a purposeful and conscious relationship between and among distinct groups, individuals, or platforms. Networks in virtual organizations serve primarily to facilitate the sharing of information and access to resources or opportunities.

Parallel, Sequential, and Pooled Work: Parallel work is work performed by individuals independently, simultaneous or not, and later integrated into a final product. Sequential work occurs one person or group at a time until a point of completion, then "handed off" to the next person or group, and so on until the work is completed. It functions much as a manufacturing assembly line. Pooled sequential work is a system where work/products are "checked in and checked out," like a library book. It is not a pure "hand off"; the same hands may touch the work multiple times at different points of its development. All know where the work is "stored" for retrieval.[10]

"Push, Pull, or Post" Knowledge: In a knowledge management process, individuals or groups can "push" information out to people, whether asked for or expected. For example, company bulletins or newsletters can be "pushed" through broadcast fax, email, videoconference, and other methods of one-way, outgoing communication.

---

[9]Rudy L. Ruggles, *Knowledge Management Tools,* 3rd ed. (Boston: Butterwork-Heinemann Press, 1997).
[10]Deborah Duarte and Nancy Tennant Snyder, *Mastering Virtual Teams* (San Francisco: Jossey-Bass Publishers, 1999).

When someone "pulls" information, he is going to a resource and "pulling" the data out of a database or other resource. Asking a mentor to pick her brain is an example of pulling information. Doing a database or Internet search pulls information. Putting out a request for assistance through a community of practice network pulls information.

Posting is just what it sounds like. Information is "posted" for general viewing. The age-old cork bulletin board is a posting methodology, as is the more current electronic bulletin board. Project or departmental web sites are often great sources for posted information, available to those who seek it but not forced on anyone, as pushed information is.

Systems Thinking: At its broadest level, systems thinking looks at the interrelatedness of forces and sees them as part of a common process. The field includes cybernetics and chaos theory, gestalt therapy, and process mapping flows. All of these approaches have one guiding idea in common: that the behavior of all systems follows certain common principles, the nature of which are being explored and applied in organizational settings.[11] To simplify, an organization functions much more like the human body with all its organic intricacies, rather than the common comparison to a machine with "cogs." Just as we humans are more than the sum of our parts, so are organizations.

Systemic Structure: Some people think the "structure" of an organization is the organization chart. Others think "structure" means the design of organizational workflow and processes. In systems thinking, the "structure" is the pattern of interrelationships among key components of the system. That might include the hierarchy and process flows, but it also includes attitudes and perceptions, the quality of products, the ways in which decisions are made, and hundreds of other factors. Systemic structures are often invisible—until someone points them out. If you ask yourself questions such as: "What happens if it changes?" you begin to see that every element is part of one or more systemic structures.[12]

---

[11]Adapted from Senge, et al., *The Fifth Discipline Fieldbook.*
[12]Senge, et al., *The Fifth Discipline Fieldbook.*

Synchronous and Asynchronous: Again, Merriam-Webster defines synchronous as:

1. happening, existing, or arising at precisely the same time
2. recurring or operating at exactly the same periods
3. of, used in, or being digital communication (as between computers) in which a common timing signal is established that dictates when individual bits can be transmitted, in which characters are not individually delimited, and which allows for very high rates of data transfer

Collaborative tools and work may be synchronous (same time), such as live Internet-based training using streaming video, electronic whiteboards, and interactive software. Other collaborative tools are asynchronous only (different time), such as email, voicemail, and CD-Rom training. Some tools may be delivered synchronously and captured for review or modified later for asynchronous use.

2

VIRTUAL IS VIABLE

REFRAMING THE ORGANIZATION, ENVIRONMENT, AND CULTURE

Will the future ever arrive? Should we continue to look upwards? Is the light we can see in the sky one of those which will presently be extinguished? The ideal is terrifying to behold, lost as it is in the depths, small, isolated, a pinpoint, brilliant but threatened on all sides by the dark forces that surround it; nevertheless, no more in danger than a star in the jaws of the clouds.

—Victor Hugo

Potential must either unite, integrate, create, and multiply, or it will isolate, disintegrate, and die.

—Kathleen Hurly and Theodore Dobson

We have it in our power to begin the world again.
—Thomas Paine, Common Sense, 1776

Jeffrey, the CEO of Fast Growth Company Inc. (FGC), met with a key strategic partner and was excited about an opportunity but nervous about the turnaround time. He called the office from his car, calling all to arms—powwow in the conference room in 15 minutes. All priorities were realigned. When Jeffrey walked through the door, the coffee was brewing, the whiteboard was wiped clean, the team was assembled minus Marianne (still at lunch), and the meeting began. Thirty minutes later, the team continued in a huddle, mindmapping and assigning pieces. Marianne returned, reviewed the whiteboard, rolled up her sleeves, and dove in. Jeffrey left for a customer meeting.

Two hours later, Jeffrey returns to find the team scattered to their various offices, on the phones and the computers. All have agreed to reconvene at 5:30 P.M. Jeffrey stops in Marianne's office to make sure she's fully briefed. He then remembers that Cranton needs some figures to run a spreadsheet, so he pulls the data and carries the hard copy and zip disk over to Cranton's office. Cranton isn't there, so Jeffrey writes a quick note on a post it, and leaves the material on top of the keyboard.

At 5:30, everyone scurries into the conference room and debriefs. Copies are being handed out, and everyone has at least a tree's worth of paper in front of them. All are making notes on their own copies. (Everyone hopes all are making similar notes.) The next assignments are relegated based on revisions. A project manager is assigned to compile the pieces into one flowing whole. Because of the company's fast growth, the team agrees to the short straw method, because it will mean someone pulling another really late night in order to meet the deadline. All agree it's worth it, the pay off could be spectacular, and secretly hope they get to eat at home tonight. Because of past experience, a second straw is pulled for the proofreader, who promises to be in by 6:30 A.M. in order to make sure that the deliverable report makes sense to the rested eye.

Everyone goes back to his or her computers, working in parallel. All input their revisions and deliver hard copies and disks to the short straw project manager. Many offer to be available if needed, while crossing their fingers. Jeffrey has to catch a plane to make a key presentation for additional funding and will be unavailable after noon tomorrow, so the document has to be in his hands by 11:15 A.M. to approve. All nod their heads, look at their watches, and count their stock options in their heads instead of sheep in their beds.

And so it goes.

FGC is fast growth, fast paced. The culture is highly collaborative out of necessity—and habit. Meetings, paper, more meetings, more paper and long hours at high speed are the norm. How might virtual teaming and collaborative technology change this company? Would it improve it or interfere with the focused energy?

This chapter explores how to help an organization develop virtual work without sacrificing the culture. Virtual work does invite change, however. It is naïve to think that vitual work does not impact your culture, or that your culture will not impact virtual work.

For example, one extremely large, global manufacturer is still family-owned, and the face-to-face, family feel to the business still pervades. Voicemail is not even a common tool, yielding to the age-old habit of walking to people's cubicles to talk. The business-to-business sales division was extremely unprofitable because their product distributors were often small retail stores in rural areas. Account representatives spent a great deal of time driving from retail store to retail store, losing much productive time. When the executive leadership decided to have account managers do more virtual relationship management, especially using the telephone, account representatives were quite hesitant. This was not the way to build and maintain relationships, especially in a face-to-face culture. Three months after implementing a partially virtual solution, these same account representatives were the biggest advocates of virtual work. They had watched their sales figures grow exponentially (in some cases 100 percent), and their customers were thrilled with the new arrangement. Virtual work was a success, and everyone was happy.

Because of the productivity gains and the employee and customer satisfaction, the strategic decision, naturally, was to expand the initiative to company headquarters. The in-person communication patterns were so entrenched at headquarters, however, that the people just were not ready. Luckily, the executives elected to conduct a virtual work readiness assessment first, and it was determined that, culturally, they just were not ready for a full-blown virtual work initiative. They decided to back off the original plan and begin adjusting systems and habits slowly so that the close-knit family feel to the culture could be preserved while building readiness for virtual work.

Virtual work was not abandoned as an idea. Its focus and implementation schedule was adjusted so that the culture and the change could cooperate rather than compete. You can facilitate not only change but improvement through virtual work, and do this without paralyzing the organization. If moving in a more virtual direction is strategically intelligent or driven by market demands, honoring and gently nudging your organization onto the virtual path can be the only reasonable choice.

The technical possibilities available change the way we work and the way our organizations work. Many successful fully or partially virtual organizations have paved the way for the rest, and they have found the culture and organizational environment are critical to not getting lost in cyberspace. This chapter encourages the nudge, as well as suggests how to get started.

If virtual, how might Jeffrey's company have achieved the same synergy, met the same turnaround target, achieved the same commitment, but allowed more efficiency? What if the team's meeting was online with a shared whiteboard that all could save to their hard drives when finished? What if, after assignments, all dropped their sections into one master document, available to all to be self-responsible for a writing flow and consistency across sections? What if one email or instant message notified all team members when a member's section is available for review? What if the short straw project manager becomes the authority on document management, instead of having to become a copywriter to guarantee "one voice"? How might that make his task easier? What if Jeffrey didn't need to access the figures, but Cranton could go into the network and pull them as he needs? What if Jeffrey could upload the document as many times as he desires instead of waiting literally until the eleventh hour before seeing the finished product? Would his fear of loss of control be less?

Organizational Paradigms in Recent History

Business has gone through at least three major transformations, beginning with the agrarian age of farming. The work was located where the farm was, the market was local (until mass transportation and refrigeration made distant markets viable), and the technology was the horse and plow or tractor. The primary asset was land.

The industrial age was built around the factory, also local, and the technology was the machine. The primary asset was capital equipment. Work was standardized, and factories focused on the Taylor model of efficiency and repetitive work leading to high productivity and quality control.

Certain unexamined "beliefs" defined the work environment, such as a workspace belonging to one person or family. Work happened at that workspace. The more successful one is, the bigger and better the workspace or farm. Clients and visitors were duly impressed.

In the last 40 years, the information/knowledge age has redefined the business environment. The technology of the computer era has developed "the corporation," work has become nonlocalized, and the primary asset is intellectual capital. Knowledge-based work is more social in nature, more creative, innovative, and ever evolving.

Management in many organizations, however, continues to strive for standardized work, which is abhorrent to many professionals and may, in fact, be antithetical to knowledge-based work. Organizations seem to gravitate toward imposing a command and control structure on new technology despite the inappropriate fit. We have gone beyond talking about the "information age" and have transitioned into and embraced this era as the "knowledge age." Organizational systems, structures, and cultures need to evolve to reflect congruence with the times.

The unexamined "beliefs" about the work environment have seriously undermined people's willingness to embrace virtual work as much as fear of loss of control. In a virtual organization, one person may have no "designated" workspace, or may have multiple workspaces. Work is an ongoing event based on need, not place. The workspace becomes a resource, not a status symbol.

The Nudge Needed Isn't Always a Big One, But . . .
Beliefs and Habits

FGC is a perfect company for partially virtual work, yet it continues to function from the old and unexamined "beliefs" about the work environment and workflow. Despite its progressive actions regarding strategic alliances, global marketplace with speed, and aggressive strategy, the team still revolves around meetings, paper, and parallel workflow with designated integration points.

The templates to shift habits and beliefs are available. Strategic alliances, outsourcing, and telecommuting have paved the way for new pathways of workflow collaboration. Beliefs have already adjusted regarding how to manage outside alliances. For example, when Microsoft bought Vermeer (maker of Front Page), they moved immediately into a virtual teaming structure, and, using their own product, they set up an internal web page. This became a key vehicle for educating, informing, and capturing learning. Everyone had access not only to read the page, but to add material. Even though this little company was suddenly part of a huge conglomeration, they managed the transition *virtually* while retaining a close-knit family feel. Everyone felt they knew what was going on, and they could help keep others informed as well.

Many companies are already outsourcing noncore functions. FGC, for example, outsources its human resource, marketing, and public relations functions. In such strategic alliances, focus is placed less on power and hierarchy, and more on the relationship and agreements between the companies. Agreements are contractual, but also often value-driven. Outsourcers are selected based on compatible approaches, values, and their ability to reflect a similar image to customers, especially if the alliance includes client work or client management.

Is this anything new, really? It may not be an embedded model in typical corporations yet, but the model has solidly succeeded in other environments. Think of the team created in the movie industry. The "team" is built around the movie, and consists of team members that are highly interactive and interdependent—producers, director, screenwriters, actors, cinematographers, musicians, and so on. Rather than literal boxes and silos, as in a traditional organization chart, networked teams are created based on virtual circles or webs.

Multiple Teams in a Silo Environment

Team members in many organizations are members of multiple teams and, therefore, have multiple alliances. Special committees, task forces, and cross-functional project teams often require team members to carry the additional role of "representative" to and for another part of the organization. In such teams, it has been my experience that the team members' primary alliances are to their "home" team, and the other team commitments are often seen as auxiliary. Interestingly, these other team commitments are also often virtual, even if everyone is co-located on the same work campus. "Representation" often takes on a feeling of protection, advocacy, and politicking. If the organization supports and reinforces a traditional, functional silo model, this will continue. It can interfere with team members' commitment to and identification with multiple teams.

This is a cultural issue more than a team-specific issue. Realistically, however, many organizations are still at least partially working from a traditional, functionally driven paradigm. Virtual team leaders who have members with multiple alliances may need to assist members in navigating multiple priorities. Teams are part of larger systems, and team members are often part of other teams. They must be able to network not only with themselves, but also with other teams, the larger organization, and its alliances. You cannot build networked organizations on electronic networks alone; the culture must also be network-driven.

It's the connections of people and technology that makes collaboration easy and sustainable. Communication and connection is, in fact, where most of the actual process of work gets done. A Harvard Business School study[13] conducted over five years studied complex and dynamic businesses that were undergoing radical changes, often rather unsuccessfully. Businesses studied ranged from Nike to Royal Dutch Shell. They found that an organization is fundamentally a social structure. It may be motivated for various reasons, but the workflow to achieve strategic objectives is always driven by social interactions that are shaped by the social structure.

What they also found was that "despite this clearly relational nature of the concept, however, an increasing preoccupation with structural forms has resulted in most organizational analysis focusing not on the network of roles and relationships that define a social structure but on constructs such as centralization, formalization, or divisionalization which, at best, represent some broad generalizations about those relationships." In other words, social relationships are the fuel of organizations, but organizations continue to attempt control through structure, which often inhibits collaborative relationships. Maybe good intentions, but the focus is misplaced.

---

[13]BEYOND THE M-FORM: Toward a Managerial Theory of the Firm. Christopher Bartlett, Professor of Business Administration, Harvard Business School and Sumantra Ghoshal, Professor of Strategy and Management, INSEAD. Internet document.

If social interaction in your organization flows through hierarchy, power, and silo, expect more challenge in becoming a truly network- and collaboratively driven organization. Focus, perhaps, on assisting people, teams, and departments in creating new "habits" of interaction that share knowledge, repeated consistently over time. Then the habit becomes part of the social structure of the organization. You will be learning to become a learning organization, and preparing the organization for a virtual environment.

A virtual work readiness assessment described later in this chapter and included in the appendix will assist you in determining how and where to start shaping your organization's culture to support networked interaction. Networked interaction supports virtual work, and vice versa. Virtual work then is a smooth, sustainable, and invisible fabric in the organization's culture. Chapter 4 discusses in more depth the systemic considerations in pursuing a virtual work environment.

Organization Design That Supports a Virtual Environment

In addition to systems and processes, the physical design of a building can support or deter a collaborative organizational fabric. Create many small, private workspaces, called hotelling. As in a Hotel Hilton, an employee can come in, get a "room," and that can be his or her work-station for the day, week, or month. Some companies have lockers for employees to keep personal items, favorite supplies, and other relevant "stuff" that they can carry to their workstation. The workstation is plug-and-play—a computer terminal or docking station, Internet con- nection, and appropriate peripherals.

Have many teaming rooms of various sizes and grandeur or infor- mality. Office furniture manufacturers have furniture lines designed for on-the-fly redesign. Tables can be joined together to form a conference table and pulled apart to form smaller table groups. Audio conferenc- ing and/or videoconferencing capabilities should be available in several teaming rooms. Whiteboards are electronic and tied into collaborative software, if virtual team members will be conferencing in to the meet- ing, or if the team wants to "capture and save" the boarded work. Have some rooms that are void of technology, just for old times sake.

A teaming room may be a training session in the morning for 17 people and a project team meeting in the afternoon, housing five.

Create an organizational design that encourages a virtual teaming environment, which is amorphous and more group-centered when together on-site. As your organization plans for its own future, facilities should morph to fit your evolving culture.

A Culture of Independence and Control

Having teams work collaboratively requires a shift in the business emphasis from "me" to "us." Training in collaborative tools is only half the solution. The other half is to develop and reward collaborative environments.

Recently, a global consulting firm examined its own culture for evidence of collaboration, knowledge sharing, and effective use of collaborative tools. They found embarrassingly little cooperation with peers until the partner level. What they found, in fact, was an extremely competitive and individualistic operating norm. Upon investigation, rewards, compensation, and career pathing did not support collaboration, even though the firm had invested heavily in collaborative tools. The tools were used as personal organizational tools, but were no more effective than the simplest shareware available on the Internet.

The corporate mantra for years has been team and cooperation, but it won't take hold if the unspoken belief is in lone ranger heroes. Business biographies reinforce this belief. Recruitment policies and packages reinforce this belief. Performance appraisal processes reinforce this belief. What does *your* organization reinforce?

Can You Say, "The Emperor Has No Clothes"?

Very few organizations stand up to the scrutiny. Very few individuals stand up to the scrutiny. Everyone has a belief system, a habit, an enculturation or two that interferes with our ability to be fully effective. Everyone. So don't wait to get started. All great journeys begin with the first step. So, you ask, which comes first—changing your culture to fit the virtual environment, or virtual teaming to lead the charge for a more collaborative culture? BOTH. They feed and support one another.

A publishing company[14] that is committed to telecommuting, one form of virtual work, does not have a culture that is "100 percent ready" for virtual work, yet they have a successful and sustaining telework initiative in place that is a few years old. For example, they have some means for document sharing, but not for their primary publishing production software. The editors and graphics designers work on their hard drives at their home offices, then transport the documents between the home office via zip or jaz cartridges. In addition, when an editor or graphics designer who is a telecommuting virtual worker has to have their documents reviewed by someone who works on-site, they must make a trip to the downtown location to perform those checks. This does minimize the productivity gains that some companies with more advanced technology realize. On the other hand, this cost-efficient measure allowed the company to implement a virtual program where telecommuting virtual workers were not required to provide their own computers and the organization was not required to make immediate, significant investments in infrastructure that would have slowed down their implementation. Some managers address this by using couriers and delivery services.

While this may seem like a limited solution, it has yielded several benefits. They state that they have been able to hire and retain employees that otherwise would not have come to work for the organization, or who would have terminated their employment. There are approximately 65 fewer offices required at the downtown location. Managers have testified that the morale among virtual workers has improved, and virtual workers have cut many hours of commute time from their schedules, resulting in a better balance in their lives as well as increased productivity.

Companies have to address the reality of incorporating remote work and teams with their current cultures based on a team concept. The dynamic tension will be greater or less, depending on the gap between an organization's current culture and a virtual, collaborative culture. This publishing company is a testament to success despite beginning in less than perfect conditions. Many readers will be in

---

[14]Many thanks to LifeWay Christian Resources for being so generous with their time and their data.

organizations like the publishing company that are not going to whole-sale rearrange themselves overnight. Use them as an example, and commit to getting started anyway.

Given that reality, it still helps build success if change leaders have a clear understanding of the driving and restraining forces for virtual work, based on the organization's core culture. Dr. Bill Schneider's extensive and ongoing work on corporate cultures finds that every organization operates primarily from one of four core cultures.[15]

Collaboration Culture

A collaborative organization builds its culture based on the idea of the family or an athletic team. It values synergy, egalitarianism, and harmony. Its leadership approach is that of coaching and team building. The market strategy is to satisfy unique needs through establishing customer intimacy. Learning and training are primarily on-the-job experience, and the organization moves ahead based on the collective learning of and sharing by its employees and its customers.

Since collaborative cultures naturally team and naturally flex to a changing marketplace, they are more ideally suited and naturally aligned for extending to a virtual environment. If the organization relies heavily on on-the-job training, extending training and development into a virtual environment may require adjustments, but the natural philosophy and affinity will support virtual work's success.

Competence Culture

Competence cultures are built from the socialization base of educational organizations, particularly the university. They value achievement, professionalism, innovation, and collective and individual competence. These organizations build relationships internally and externally based on task and competence, and they pride themselves on providing the best products and services available, and by taking a leadership position in the marketplace based on excellence. Information and knowledge are shared to produce superior products and

[15]For more information on core cultures see William Schneider, *Reengineering Alternative: A Plan for Making Your Current Culture Work* (Burr Ridge, IL: Irwin Publishing, 1994).

services, learning is about developing expertise, and training tends to support the development and expansion of job competencies.

Competence cultures value tool usage that enables the organization to serve the customer and be the best, most elite organization in the marketplace, and are open to trying "new things" that will expand their expertise. Virtual work supports a global marketplace competitive edge, so collaborative cultures are conducive to embracing the virtual paradigm. Teams in competence cultures are also built on expertise and competence, and are used to developing swift trust. Therefore, competence cultures have less difficulty adapting to a virtual environment.

Cultivation Culture

Cultivation cultures are modeled after religious organizations and believe that they and their people will do what they value. They strive to transcend current limits and achieve a meaningful purpose. They value creativity, dedication, and belief in their own mission. Leaders in cultivation cultures are catalysts and stewards. Their market strategy is to enrich and assist in fulfilling customers' potential. The rightness of the organization's vision and values prevail, and information and knowledge are shared to further the nobility of the vision. Emphasis is placed upon group growth and development in service to the organization's purpose.

Cultivation cultures focus on developing people and projects fully. This value will lend itself well to developing "cyber communities" and virtual teams. On the other hand, while cultivation can be done virtually, it often requires a shift in mental models for people used to developing people in a more traditional, hands-on, mentoring fashion.

Control Culture

Control cultures build their organizations based on the military armed services. Bureaucracies are born here. Control cultures like to "capture" market share through operational excellence. They value certainty, discipline, objectivity, order, and structure. Leadership tends to be more authoritative and directive, and roles and position carry weight. Their market strategy leans toward providing the best price with the least inconvenience by being streamlined and efficient. The framework for sharing information, training, and learning is built around the business strategy, business metrics, core processes, and results.

Control cultures probably struggle the most with virtual environments until they find the processes and infrastructure to help them keep a reign on things. They are the last to embrace a work environment that loosens the controls. On the other hand, control cultures are competitively driven and want to "capture" the marketplace. Being globally accessible through virtual work is very motivating. If a control culture can harness efficient virtual processes without interfering with the essential flux and free flow required in a virtual environment, it can succeed very well virtually. It will also be more likely to provide tested and proven support and efficiency aids to virtual workers than the other three cultures.[16]

As you can see, all organizational cultures are more *and* less conducive to virtual work and virtual teams. It's not about which culture is better, it's about identifying what in the culture supports virtual work, and what requires more effort and patience. Regardless of an organization's core culture, strive for the following responsibilities, shared by everyone regardless of status, longevity, or experience:

- ✓ Build trust instead of suspicion, and value sharing over secrecy.
- ✓ Achieve the end product; no one "hands off" responsibility until the goal is achieved.
- ✓ Seek and provide information and knowledge. No one can be excused because she "didn't get the memo."
- ✓ Create meaningful work.
- ✓ Leverage learning across the entire organization and strategic alliances.

How Naked Is the Emperor?

To know how big the gap is between your vision of a virtual culture and your organization's current culture, conduct a top down/bottom up assessment of virtual teaming as a viable workplace strategy. Look at current organizational, strategic, operational, managerial, employee, technical, and productivity measurement readiness and preparedness.

---

[16]For more information on core cultures see William Schneider, *Reengineering Alternative: A Plan for Making Your Current Culture Work.*

For those organizations already partially virtual, also assess the consistency with which virtual work is being implemented across divisions, departments, facilities, and teams. An honest examination identifies strategic issues and opportunities in expanding a virtual environment. See the appendix for a template to build your own virtual organizational readiness assessment questionnaire.

Technology's Role in Setting Culture

Culture is maintained through communication, connection, and shared agreements about "how we really do things around here." Technology has always played a role in creating and maintaining organizational culture. The technology of the pen and paper were predominant connectors prior to the telephone. The telephone was predominant prior to email. Previous technologies do not go away; the cadre of available tools merely expands. At first a new technology seems strange or unnecessary, then it becomes indispensable. The more we use technology, the more it becomes a transparent, necessary tool, like a flipchart easel or whiteboard. Who remembers having only one telephone number? Now we have voice, fax, voicemail, wireless, pagers, email forwarded to wireless, voicemails forwarded to emails, and on it goes. I find it ironic that the latest technology is networking all the vehicles together back into "one number, one destination."

One can certainly argue for overload, but one cannot argue against the tools themselves. Competence with collaborative tools is hardly an option; it has become expected. We now view virtual modes of communication as vital as face-to-face, and often superior. Where asynchronous communication is needed, virtual tools rise to the occasion, all this without losing the value or place for face-to-face.

*The technology is a powerful enabler and becomes better every day. Real collaboration is still about people and not a self-maintaining, technical function. Healthy collaboration is a function of people's intentions and commitments; the tools become the mechanisms used to perpetuate a collaborative culture and fulfill commitments. Intention, commitment, trustworthiness, task completion—these are still the critical components of a healthy organizational structure, and these components are **people** components.*

Yet to say that the connectivity infrastructure is neutral is also inaccurate. Their value is in the way in which they help people, systems, and networks. Ask anyone whose hard drive is crashed or who has not been able to access the network at a critical time, and he will tell you how vital the technology has become. Networks—technical and people— work together for the whole.

Reframing Old Terms with New Meaning

So far this chapter has focused on the organization culture. Virtual teams develop their own cultures as well. While every team member takes on a commitment to support and sustain the team and its relationship to the organization, the team leader has particular responsibilities to create a culture that works for his team. Team facilitation is an ongoing commitment, including the time spent together in person or virtually and the time spent between meetings. The social relationships are no less important within the virtual team than they are in the organization. The knowledge management technology—interactive databases, search engines, filters—facilitate collaboration and learning, but it is still how a team weaves its own social fabric that determines real and lasting success.

Virtual team members need to be competent in both face-to-face and virtual environments, and synchronous and asynchronous modes of communication and facilitation. Deep commitment and caring is created not just by spending "real time" together; they can be created through virtual methods as well. Different modes of connection can create effective interaction. Other chapters dedicated to building emotional bandwidth (trust) and communication develop this further. For now, though, let's define four terms.

1. Common (Virtual) Ground

People tend to attach to people with whom they share common ground. Common ground is "a basis for mutual interest or agreement."[17] A team certainly qualifies as common work ground, but commitment is deepened when the team actually feels that it is a sort of temporary

---

[17]*Merriam-Webster's Collegiate Dictionary,* 10th ed., 1998.

"community" with shared purpose and responsibilities, rituals and habits, successes and challenges, and history. A team leader needs to help the team intentionally design opportunities to develop shared experience together.

When a team is virtual, it has a more difficult time seeing itself as a whole that is moving together toward a common goal. The communication infrastructure and ground rules help, but it's also important to help each member *know* every part of this "whole" team, *know* their common ground, so that everyone sees how individual actions contribute to forward movement, sees how individuals impact the collective.

Imagine a mobile. Each team member dangles from a wire, and the wires connect the team members together into a beautiful and flowing creation. Often the mobile pieces never touch, but they still "flow" together without effort. The team leader needs to make sure the "wires" connect the team so that they are not isolated pieces that never come together to create more than the sum of their parts. This synergy, this "wiring" of individuals together through creating common ground, is what makes teams so powerful. The intention is to assist every member to feel like an individual and a manifestation of the whole.

Is there a metaphor or analogy that your team can create that symbolically wires you together powerfully enough to remind everyone at all times *why you are together?*

The team leader is creating a culture that supports relationships, not just hands off tasks. Sharing personal and virtual office photographs, individual web pages, personal and professional victories and celebrations, and other vehicles help create common ground. It also helps to facilitate deep conversation that is not directly related to the project or team mission. Deep conversation is not always automatic, even for co-located teams. Team leaders can facilitate opportunities by providing intentional common ground, such as discussion topics, guest lecturers, team training, or other shared experiences.

2. Sacred (Virtual) Space

Remember the last time you were in a meeting when the group was synergistic, the creativity was flowing, and you could feel the energy bouncing off the walls? One question led to the next brainstorm, which led to the next improvement, which led to a breakthrough approach. Going to lunch or ordering in just builds the charge even more. Perhaps you are one of the lucky ones who have a team experience where this high energy is the norm. The room or "space" itself seems to hold the energy of the group, forming a sort of container, just as a glass holds water or a pocket holds personal effects. Understandably, one should not recklessly abandon such a sacred space, that holding of the team energy in place.

Virtual teams can experience a sort of energy leak, like the glass got tipped over, if sacred virtual space isn't created and nurtured. Team leaders need to be concerned about creating, containing, and modulating team energy. Energy cannot be at full throttle all the time; the team would burn out. If the ebb and flow, however, isn't managed, the risk of a virtual environment is too much dissipation, resulting in lagging commitment or focus. Practical mechanisms that help are virtual water coolers, ICQ (a way to see who else on the team is online at the time), open and ongoing chat rooms, instant messaging, electronic bulletin boards, and virtual and face-to-face team meetings focused on relationship building.

Each type of interaction can be its own container, and creating that intentionally helps build and hold the energy of the group appropriately. For example, a one-on-one conversation with instant messaging has a more intimate feeling than a team meeting, including the fact that there is usually no recorded history of the conversation. Free flowing conversation affords a kind of freedom to speak that threaded listserves do not. If an entire conversation is recorded, some people will be less forthright in their conversation. Electronic whiteboard brainstorming can stimulate group synergy much as a physical room can, especially if shared metaphors and stories abound.

Just as a kitchen feels cozier than a formal dining room, or a meditation space has a quieter feel than a living room, different "workspaces" hold different senses. Different "spaces" have different boundaries and expectations. An office with a closed door suggests heads down, focused work that should not be disturbed. An open door with colleagues laughing provides a different sense. Teams can create virtual clues for one another to sense the "room" one is entering. For example, a team may typically hold one of three types of meetings—new client development strategies, project specific, and organizationally focused. When a meeting is called, the caller can indicate through a pre-determined icon what type of meeting it is. Project meetings, for example, may be symbolized by a toolbox. The toolbox indicates a working session, and everyone brings his or her contributions with the expectation that something will be accomplished.

One last aspect of sacred space also needs mentioning. The team exists, even when it isn't electronically or personally connected. Team leaders hold the space with the group between connections, assuring that the sacred space continues regardless of who is currently "in the virtual room." For example, I participate with a learning group annually for three days. During those three days, we physically share sacred space, living together in community and pursuing professional conversation together. Between annual gatherings, several of us continue our sense of presence and connectedness through emails, a threaded online community, and subgroups meeting and conversing at deeper levels through various media, including face to face. The "place" of our gathering is a great treat for us, but the "sacred space" of our commitment and connection is always "there," even when we are not present or communicating frequently.

3. *Virtual Team Spirit*

The energy is built, the space is set, and now the team needs to keep the fires burning. When those two team members have their heads together and hit a "Eureka!" moment, they need to run virtually to the whole group and share the excitement. Then. Not later. Broadcast fax or email or voicemail. Seek teammates through ICQ. Let the enthusiasm show in the voice, the exclamation points, and the words. When Jeffrey's now virtual team hits the mark, Jeffrey can celebrate by having pizzas and beer delivered to everyone's virtual office. When a team member receives a special award, find ways to feature her in a video clip or email press release. Develop a habit of posting fun and exciting news to a team bulletin board or team web page. Develop the additional habit of high-fiving people back, always responding positively to acknowledge the accomplishment. Celebrate accomplishments as a team together, even when disbursed. And celebrate again when you are together. No team can be too spirited, whether virtual or co-located. Do a virtual jig. Send e-cards. Send songs. Have fun. It's a good thing.

4. *Expanding Emotional Bandwidth*

The next chapter focuses on expanding emotional bandwidth, or trust, with your team. Not to sound redundant, but implementing the technology is the easy part. Building the relationships, however, is where the real power is. At the team level, simple conversation is the single most powerful strategy for building emotional bandwidth. Face-to-face, juicy emails, telephone conversations, online conferences, all support the value in simply spending time together, collectively and in subgroups. Frequent "check-ins," perhaps even daily, should be the norm. I'm not suggesting, "Goodnight, Mary Ellen. Goodnight, Johnboy," but it couldn't hurt. . . . Besides, simple conversation between or among individuals is how most organizational learning gets done. Knowledge management systems, however well deployed, can never replace the learning that occurs in simple conversation. As a committed team member or leader, keep the conversations going.

3

EXPANDING EMOTIONAL BANDWIDTH

Building Trust in the Virtual Team

We shall never be able to remove suspicion and fear as potential causes of war until communication is permitted to flow, free and open, across international boundaries.

—*Harry S. Truman*

Few things can help an individual more than to place responsibility on him, and to let him know that you trust him.

—*Booker T. Washington*

This chapter reexamines what we know, and think we know, about trust in teams. This is one area of virtual work that is primarily people dependent. The establishing of trust will not be sped up by better technology. Today we have available almost unlimited bandwidth, but what about emotional bandwidth? How do we broaden our faith in and dependable commitment to one another as interdependent team members? The technology supports communication and connection, but it cannot drive commitment or trust. The social and work agreements are built, and the mechanisms are tools to fulfill agreements. If agreements are met, trust is built. If excuses or failed agreements occur, what then? Trust is one of the most commonly stated barriers to virtual teaming. This chapter explores that argument.

What Do We Think We Know
about Group Dynamics and Trust?

Integrity creates a foundation for trust. "Integrity," for this book's purposes, means aligning actions with words, intent with outcome, unity with self and others. Much literature on trust suggests it is difficult if not impossible to establish trust virtually. Eyeballs are needed because trust is based on social relationships built as a result of time spent together. People who live and work near each other are assumed to share similar social traits and preferences, values and expectations, experience, and habits. This assumption carried further then is that trust will develop or erode based on experience together. Trust theory also states that first impressions count and last. Additionally, the theory goes that we are more inclined to be trustworthy, hence more trusted, when we *have* to continue to see and work with someone in the future. In other words, we follow through on commitments when we have to "face" each other again.

Theory and evidence also suggest that distance creates distance. Distance remains a very real dimension in human relations. Communication among team members drops quickly even when they are separated by only one floor or building. On the surface, this does seem to inhibit trust building in virtual teams.

While there is much evidence to support the social developmental nature of trust, it is not the only way to build trust, especially as people become more comfortable with electronic communication. Recent research and my experience sheds a much more hopeful light on virtual team trust. What does hold, though, is that first impressions count. Also, early-established patterns tend to entrench early and become deeply embedded, regardless of how ineffective they are or if better options appear. This suggests the importance of establishing trust-building habits early. This chapter will explore what trust-building habits thrive in a virtual environment.

Swift Trust

Meyerson, Weick, and Kramer[18] identified "swift trust" in groups as a trust building strategy which "de-emphasizes the interpersonal dimen-

---

[18]D. Meyerson, K. E. Weick, and R. M. Kramer, "Swift trust and temporary groups." In R. M. Kramer and T. R. Tyler, eds., *Trust in Organizations: Frontiers of Theory and Research* (Thousand Oaks, CA: Sage Publications, 1996), pp. 166–195.

sions and is based initially on broad categorical social structures and later on action." It is the professional reputation and integrity of the team members that warrant trusting each other. Trust is given, but not guaranteed to continue. It is temporary until experience proves the trust is deserved. As a result, trust may be at its height at the beginning of team formation. The trust cup starts full, and is depleted or replenished based on negative or positive experiences.

Swift trust obviously plays well in a virtual environment. It is not, however, automatic. Jarvenpaa and Leidner conducted an experimental research study that tested trust, and specifically swift trust, in a 100 percent virtual teaming environment.[19] Their findings support what I have found with clients, as well as my own experience. The implications help create a solid recipe for virtual team trust development and maintenance.[20] Among their many conclusions, they found that teams that ended the team relationship with high trust "exhibited swift, action-based trust with social communications interweaved throughout interactions. Trusting behavior may itself have provided the cognitive and emotional basis for the trust that was then maintained. In swift trust, unless one trusts quickly, one may never trust at all."

Band-Aid or Bond Aid?

The greater the group's commitment to the purpose and to the virtual environment, the more likely team members will see virtual trust as viable, and virtual teaming as no barrier to building and maintaining trust. The team's loyalty is with each other if the team functioning and teamwork is satisfying. This does not necessarily translate into an increased commitment to the larger organization, which brought the team together in the first place. Ways of ensuring organizational commitment are explored elsewhere in this book. For the purposes of expanding emotional bandwidth, however, one can say that if people begin with swift trust and are satisfied with their ongoing team interaction and teamwork, they are committed to one another. They feel a bond to the team as a whole and to members individually.[21]

---

[19]Sirkka L. Jarvenpaa and Dorothy E. Leidner, "Communication and Trust in Global Virtual Teams" (*Journal of Computer-Mediated Communication* 3(4), June 1998).

[20]I will refer frequently to Jarvenpaa and Leidner's findings in this chapter. I will, therefore, not reference by footnote each time.

[21]James Wallace Bishop and K. Dora Scott, *HRM Magazine*, SHRM Foundation Research, February 1997.

Bishop and Scott also found that the handling of conflict and level of team commitment contributed to a team's bonding. The degree of interpersonal conflict correlates with members' intention to quit. If unhealthy conflict goes undetected or unresolved for too long, team members will look around for alternatives. Trust becomes absent, or a negative trust results—"I can count on you to let me down." On the positive side, the more quickly, honestly, and respectfully interpersonal conflict is handled, the greater is the likelihood of trust being built or restored, and commitment remains high.

Again Jarvenpaa and Leidner's findings support Bishop and Scott. All virtual team members had vulnerabilities, uncertainties, and expectations, including technical difficulties. The teams that ended with low trust were less able to handle the challenges, including not being able to manage conflict effectively. They blamed each other and the technology for their problems, creating a conflict ridden and unsafe environment.

The higher the team commitment, the higher is the willingness to help one another and the higher the productivity. Not only does inter-dependency increase willingness to help one another, commitment increases willingness. Jarvenpaa and Leidner also found this to be true. Teams that began with swift trust and ended with high trust immersed themselves in the task. All showed initiative and roles emerged. They encouraged each other and contributed to each other's work.

Teams that began with high trust but watched that trust erode experienced disappointment that significantly impacted commitment and productivity. They began with initial enthusiasm and excitement about the virtual environment and their team. They believed in inter-dependence. Unfortunately, they believed in being helped more than helping. Team members waited for others to take the initiative. They were committed initially to getting to know one another, but no one shifted the group to task or took leadership initiative. As a result, commitment and trust waned.

Teams that began and ended with low trust and commitment did not change much during their project time. Team members in Jarvenpaa and Leidner's research began and ended with little optimism, excitement, or initiative. Trust, commitment, and, therefore, productivity never had a chance. Band-Aids (e.g., swift trust that gets reinforced and communication protocols) nor bond aids (e.g., conflict mangement and team satisfaction) contributed to effective functioning.

It is possible to use Band-Aids to give a jump-start to missing or diminishing trust. In Jarvenpaa and Leidner's research, teams that began with low trust but finished with high trust had a little self-created help. Members felt uncertain and were initially preoccupied with establishment of rules to manage their uncertainty—a Band-Aid of sorts. Eventually they overcame those uncertainties by focusing on task and resisting distractions. They shifted from a procedural to task focus and resolved technical difficulties together.

Since high productivity and effectiveness is the bottom line for any organization, it is a team leader's responsibility to do whatever it takes to create a work environment for productivity, trust, and effectiveness to happen. Use Band-Aids to build bonds until the bonds are strong enough to hold by themselves. These findings hold true for all teams, regardless of the work location or team location—virtual or co-located. To summarize, interdependence, coworker satisfaction, and healthy conflict management are key variables for team member trust and commitment, which leads to a high performing team.

Contextual Clues

How virtual trust gets built is impacted by whether the work culture of a team or organization is one of high context or low context. High-context cultures are situational and nonverbal cues convey primary meaning. In a virtual environment, taking extra time to give everyone a sense of "place" is more critical for high-context culture teams. A virtual team is like any community in that its culture is a product of shared stories, norms, shared rituals, repeated interactions, and shared experiences. Provide opportunities to create shared history together.

Places are spaces that are valued and hold meaning. In a high-context culture, "place" frames appropriate behavior. In a low-context culture, place is in the meaning, and meaning is conveyed primarily through written and spoken words. Space is the opportunity, and place is the understood reality.

For example, I'm a member of three online communities. All three communities use the same "space" (egroups.com), but one community is a high-context culture. For members except me, this is their first online community. It may seem odd then to say that we are the most active community of the three I belong to, and we are only about one year old. What has helped our success is the time we take to provide "context." At least one-third of our communication involves social and personal information and describing what our "worlds" are like individually. We share fun news, new business opportunities, and other personal information along with conversation about the community subject matter. Occasionally we have telephone or in-person interaction.

The other two communities are low context, and few of us know anything about each other personally. Every communication is topic-focused. As far as I know, no one has met. The only "place" these groups hold is the online community threads. Some rich exchange still occurs in these communities, but it is strictly topic-focused, and the content provides the only context.

Not all virtual teams need to spend much time on place and context, but a team leader in a high-context culture ignores this at his own peril. After all, virtual people don't populate a virtual team, real people do. People are real, engaged in real interactions in the course of doing their real work. Even low-context cultures usually increase personal commitment to the team when some context or "place" is included in the interactions.

High-context cultures often develop as a team more slowly than low-context cultures. Trust has to be established first and isn't as prone to swift trust unless encouraged to do so with backgrounds, resumes, and other vehicles to "speed up" the familiarity period. Negotiations and workflow processes tend to evolve more slowly and ritualistically, whereas in low-context cultures business is conducted quickly. For high-context cultures it becomes even more productive to find a way to hold an initial, preferably in-person, team development planning session (discussed in a later chapter) so that a modified swift trust can be established.

High-context members build trust before focusing on the tasks and in low-context cultures, the reverse is true. Trust is based on expertise, reputation, and performance. Swift trust happens more readily in a low-context culture, but can also occur in a high-context culture with guidance and assistance.

Does Your Reputation Precede You?

While reputation is a stated trust attribute in a low-context culture, it is important regardless of context. In fact, willingness to readily trust is impacted significantly by how much a team member's reputation is on the line based on actions of another team member. Trust is needed for collaboration, but there can be acceptable collaboration with low trust if the rules are clearly enough defined. If great interdependence is required and the individuals' reputations are significantly impacted by team performance, high trust is high stakes, regardless of incentive to cooperate. My advice to build and retain swift trust when reputation is at risk is to pick team members very carefully based on experience, competence, and reputation for integrity. Then follow other guidelines described here in order to be trustworthy of leading a great virtual team.

Regardless of high- or low-context culture, a few guidelines to build swift and ongoing trust prevail:

✓ Describe your context vividly and find time for some social conversation.

✓ Minimize discussion of organizational hierarchy and other "power" contexts. It sets up a tendency to defer or rely too heavily on the most "powerful."

✓ All teams have team members who hold private conversations that are not relevant to the whole. This is essential, appropriate, and helps bond team members. A fast way to splinter a virtual team, however, is to provide inappropriate context, such as a private joke or conversation. Keep private conversation private unless it is relevant to the group, in which case provide the context and background to establish relevancy and inclusion.

Give It Up, Girl (Boy)!

There is a direct relationship between trust and knowledge sharing. One context-irrelevant cultural element is how the organization supports or deters knowledge sharing. An information-hoarding organization will hamper somewhat the depth of trust that can be established in any team, and can be exacerbated in a virtual team because distant team members cannot fully "trust" that they are getting all the information they need.

The simple act of sharing information can demonstrate to other team members that a team member understands what is relevant, can summarize information and establish relevance, and trusts the team to know one's thoughts. Part of good team play is learning what information is crucial and passing it on. These are all actions that build trust! This requires designing virtual environments where all the individuals feel comfortable (and have incentives) to share what they know, and they have vehicles to share without effort.

What Organizations Can Learn about Trust from the Computer Generation

"The medium is the message," according to Bill Jensen's findings in his book, *Simplicity*.[22] This is especially true for knowledge workers and Generation Y employees. Trust with the organization is built upon media that works—tools that are easy to use, practical, timely, and time efficient. If the organization provides such tools, these workers say, "I can trust you and this company to help me work smart enough fast enough." If, however, the organization is providing antiquated or difficult-to-navigate tools, creating no supportive work environments, or forcing arduous and complicated processes that waste time or resources, they hear incongruous messages. "Despite how much we say we support you and want you to work smart, we expect you to go figure it out without us."

The impact on trust is clear. If organizations want trustworthy relationships built, they must first be trustworthy. The organization must be in integrity—doing what it says it will do, aligning resources and support with its expectations for high performance. Jensen calls this "building trust with what you build." People are on overload in today's work world, and they'll trust environments that make work easier and faster and themselves more productive.

---

[22]Bill Jensen, *Simplicity: The New Competitive Advantage in a World of More, Better, Faster* (Cambridge, MA: Perseus Press, February 2000).

Navigate the Three-Fold Path toward Trust

Chapter 5 focuses on getting virtual teams off on the right path. Getting teams up and running successfully is also a major factor in building trust. Chapter 5 will develop the tenets of a Three-Fold Path, which are briefly introduced here:

- Create a cohesive team culture.
- Support the team community.
- Produce successful outcomes.

Like Glinda in the *Wizard of Oz,* the virtual manager guides the team to "follow the yellow brick path" and provides specific guidance and support along the way. Whether it's a self-directed work team, a team with revolving leadership, or a traditional team with a virtual manager, leadership includes vigilant commitment to retaining team integrity and trust. Leaders keep the team on the path of cohesion, support, and production. Be the pathfinder for the group to make sure that the "sacred space" is held for the group and that trust continues. Virtual managers who act in a conscious manner to build trust across boundaries and to share information and power create environments in which virtual work can thrive.

The Alchemy of Trust

Since ancient times, alchemy mystics have sought to transmute base metal into gold. There may not be a panacea that turns every group into a trusting team, but there are some alchemical properties that create the right recipe for teams that have that golden hue of trust. The elixir is the base ingredient that transmutes the base metal into gold—the philosopher's stone. **Communication** *serves as the elixir of virtual trust.* The carrier is the property that conveys the essence of the goal (gold). **Performance** *is the carrier for virtual trust.* At the core of a virtual work team, performance is the essential goal. The trust alchemy must be held in a container. **Integrity,** *the alignment of actions and stated values and intentions, creates a container for trust.*

Select team members who have high integrity. Select people who don't take excessive advantage of others. Select people who are essentially honest. Select people who do what they say they will do. Find out what the person can be trusted to do and help the team create workflow and group dynamic processes that help people meet their commitments and use their competencies fully. There needs to be some reasonable respect and confidence in one another in order to trust together. This is even more so in a virtual environment because face-to-face interaction isn't there for reassurance.

The Elixir: Communication

Social and Task-Based Communication   Communication about project and task is necessary to maintain trust. Social communication that complements rather than substitutes for task communication strengthens trust. An exclusively task-focused team runs the risk of dry communication revolving around logistics, coordination, and reports. This is especially common in virtual teams if the team isn't sparked to intentionally create time and space to have regular, meaty conversation, virtual and not. Conversation can be about the purpose and direction of the project, broad or strategic implications, thought-provoking or competence-building sessions, and open-ended dialogue that goes where it will. This isn't just a nice gesture, it is invaluable for virtual teams in learning and growing and thinking together.

Again, Jarvenpaa and Leidner found that teams that ended with high trust had predictable patterns of communication, sometimes intense. Frequency was less important than predictability. Participation was fairly equal, and time was spent initially setting out roles, assignments, and workflow. After the "rules of the road" were clear, focus was primarily on task with social communication weaved throughout the teams' lives. The teams that began and ended with high trust took the time initially to introduce themselves to one another socially. All teams ending with high trust kept each other informed when one member would be offline, responded to all communications quickly, and gave rich and full feedback. They also communicated together to problem solve challenges such as technical difficulties.

The opposite was found in teams that began and ended with low trust. Little time was spent on social content; communiqués were unequally distributed and were shallow, suggesting lack of commitment. Complete communication lapses occurred, and little feedback was provided when attempts to communicate or push task were made.

Mechanics   Organize and structure communication to get work done. Asynchronous web conferencing is very effective because it is convenient while still similar to face-to-face conversation. Time passes between entries during an online discussion, but the history and relevance is clear because of the continuous thread that can be read. This interaction becomes asynchronous dialogue.

Obviously web conferencing is only one tool. What is important is to decide together how the team will demonstrate full participation in the team. How do you virtually demonstrate presence and listening (virtual head nodding)? Decide together what are the best ways to ask for clarification and verification, take time to think, offer suggestions, and ask for feedback.

Agree to ground rules for how, when, and what to post, as well as how and how fast to respond. Regardless of the structure, rules, or tools, communication needs to be clear. The norm must be clearing any confusion or misunderstanding before messages get misconstrued and unintentional trust-busting results. A virtual team needs to talk about how they will operate. They need to agree, and they need to anticipate how they want to respond to breakdowns in commitment. Suggestions for negotiating and modifying operating norms and setting communication protocols are provided in Chapter 6.

Doing this early builds a foundation for trust, as long as the mechanics are seen as servants to the process. When relied upon as a control device, it does not support or derail trust; it simply controls. Like the technology, a great structure cannot build trust if it is not used well.

Feedback and Reciprocation   Virtual team members seem to share one universal trait—a high need for quick response. "Are you out there?" is the question. People want to be reassured that they are not lost in cyberspace. It is hard to trust people you don't see or hear from on a regular basis, especially when you are depending on them. A response is a statement of commitment, involvement, and support.

Without an echo, one doesn't know if she has been heard, or heard accurately. A reciprocal response says that another person is willing to take the risk of acting on or interpreting the first person's message and if necessary, supplying the missing elements to make it understandable. If a thorough feedback response is not possible immediately, at least acknowledge receipt and commit to when feedback can be provided. With Jarvenpaa and Leidner's teams, responding behaviors were as critical as initiating behaviors.

Full Interaction   Virtual managers need to encourage communication within the network of team members. So far, we have been inferring that much communication is to the entire team. Typically, virtual team communication in a traditional hierarchical environment is either inclusive of everyone, or between a member and team leader. Unless the team culture and/or team leader create reasons and methods for subgroups to communicate, they won't.

Much communication should occur in team subsets, and it needs to be encouraged in a virtual team since the natural conversation that occurs when physically near someone doesn't happen. For example, a team manager could encourage an account manager to confer with an installation technician prior to calling on the customer, or assign three team members to install and train others in a new collaborative tool, or pair up team members to work on a marketing strategy that gets reported back to the group.

It may seem obvious, but trust is eroded when people don't talk to one another. The most underrated team building trust strategy is interaction—lots of it in full groups, pairings, and subgroups. Co-located teams interact naturally because of the physical space sharing; virtual teams don't. Virtual team members say that developing virtual relationships is satisfying and builds whole team commitment, which we have already determined enhances team performance. People are more trusting of people they know and talk to regularly. Find ways to make it happen.

Find the Team's Groove   Co-located teams naturally fall into rhythms together—coffee breaks, regularly scheduled meetings, saying good morning and good night, sometimes lunches with part or all of the team. They develop a sort of groove. Effective teams work with the groove to support their activities together. Virtual teams can and should use communication and workflow patterns to create grooves. Routines create grooves, like weekly synchronous web conferences or audio conferences, daily polls or check ins, monthly face-to-face team meetings, or any combination or other creative routine.

The Carrier: Performance

This chapter began with defining integrity as aligning actions with words, intent with outcome, unity with self and others. Simply, aligned action builds trust. A pattern of meeting obligations and commitments lets an occasional slip be just an occasional slip. Good faith efforts are appreciated. Trust comes when people follow through. It really is that simple.

4

SYSTEMIC CONSIDERATIONS

WILL IT WORK HERE?

"What could be more important than doing unimportant things? If you stop to do enough of them, you'll never get to where you're going."
"But why unimportant things?"
"Think of all the trouble it saves . . . For there's always something to do to keep you from what you really should be doing."
—*Norton Juster,* The Phantom Tollbooth

The real basic structure of the workplace is the relationship. Each relationship is itself part of a larger network of relationships. These relationships can be measured along all kinds of dimensions—from political to professional expertise. The fact is that work gets done through these relationships.
—*Michael Schrage,* No More Teams

Nowhere is change going to be more dramatic than in the way organizations function in the new millennium. "Integration" is not just hardware and software and platforms. "Integration" defines the people, the work, the communication, the very structure of organizations. While few would argue, many would state that the statement is truer than the reality. People, systems resist.

47

"Virtual work leads to chaos."
"It's okay for those high tech companies, but it won't work here."

Are these statements true or false?
False, although it depends . . .

What is *true* is that a consistent, integrated, systemic approach to virtual work will yield the best results. In virtual organizations, processes are built around information, knowledge management, and collaboration. This usually means change for most organizations, regardless. No matter how frequently full access and support is stated as a strategic priority, it is often less than ideally practiced. It doesn't have to result in a total reengineering effort, but existing delivery systems and processes in many organizations simply don't work for virtual workers, especially if they work "off campus." Many systems are set up for many people, one location—human resources and training, information systems maintenance and support, corporate communications, management supervision and interaction, team and project management.

Online learning is growing, and information services is more progressive than ever, thanks primarily to Y2K readiness measures; human resources departments use intranets more effectively than most support departments. The knowledge management industry is thriving. All in all, however, each organization needs to take an honest inventory to assess its current alignment and readiness for virtual work. If that same organization then strategically and systemically aligns its systems and processes for co-located and virtual work, chaos can be avoided.

Teams can work virtually with little systemic cooperation, but their success will be hampered if the supporting organizational systems and structures are not aligned for a virtual environment. This chapter discusses organization systemic realignments and considerations in moving from a traditional organizational structure to a networked, collaborative structure. Criteria for technology and software selection are also discussed.

Organization Realignments and Considerations—New Vistas

Building community in the workplace is viewed by most as an ideal, but it doesn't need to be. If the relationships among people are the actual process of work, virtual teams open an opportunity to redefine relationships across boundaries by utilizing networks fully. Virtual teams are part of larger organizations, communities within a larger community. Rather than creating more distance, collaborative tools enable organizations to build relationships within and among teams by using relationships as the connection, rather than proximity.

The key to a successful virtual work implementation is aligning the four critical success factors through integration and systemic collaboration. The four critical success factors (CSF) are:

✓ Technology

✓ Work environment

✓ Business processes

✓ People

All four CSF's are examined and aligned from the perspective of networked collaboration. The organizational model looks more like a spider web than a silo. People are aligned with projects and customers, rather than functional departments. Electronic communication and networks, rather than hierarchy, form the backbone of the infrastructure. Work environment, business processes, systems, and infrastructure support and reward full involvement, full access to whoever is relevant—regardless of title. All strategic partners and stakeholders are connected—suppliers, workers, customers and markets, contractors, even competitors.

Not every organization, however, is ready to fully leap into a web metaphor. They may, in fact, feel caught in a web if leapt into without preparation. Virtual work can and does succeed in more traditional organizations and those in transition, although the distributed global economy is forcing many organizations in a direction that is more permeable. Virtual work is a big right step in the global direction.

Ready, Set, Jump?

Unless you are truly virtual—and few are—it is wise to assess the readiness, willingness, and ability of your organization to work and team virtually. Assessing your organization's people, technology, work environment and culture, systems and processes almost always results in virtual work as a ripe option. An honest assessment will give you more than that, however. You will also discover how quickly to grow your "virtual work web," where it will work best first, where it would fail without preparation, where the resistance and challenges are, and data to create a systemically sound plan for full relationship-managed, integrated, collaboratively networked, virtual work.

Readiness is the organization's literal preparedness for a virtual work environment. It's like a runner that is posed at the starting line waiting for the gun to go off. **Willingness** has to do with desire. **Ability** is just that—capability of the infrastructure, systems, processes, and people to operate virtually. Readiness, willingness, and ability across the four critical success factors may not be the same. For example, the technology may be ready and in place. The systems and processes may be ready with a few revisions. Growth has created a cramped office and the organization needs to expand without walls (telecommuting, for example) or lease more space. Information systems and the knowledge management folks may want it, while legal mildly resists due to security and liability concerns. The discomfort of cramped quarters may have increased people's willingness to try something new. Employees may desire more flexibility in their work/home balance.

Yet people are still reticent. The company's culture may have a family feel—birthdays and anniversaries are celebrated in the break room, meetings are always in person, and relationships often extend beyond the workday. How will virtual work impact this culture? The mindsets of the people are not prepared for a dramatic change. This does not mean virtual work is dead in the water; it does mean an honest assessment of people's readiness presents a clear picture of how, when, where, and how fast and extensively to implement virtual work.

Taking the time to do some homework will pay for itself by helping the organization do some honest self-assessment regarding how aligned it is with a greater move toward virtual work. Table 4.1 provides a template for building your organization's virtual work/team self-assessment.

Most questions can be answered with a little research, a little digging, and some targeted questions to specific functions. The greatest resource for *real* answers, however, may well lie with the organizational

Table 4.1 Organizational Self-assessment for Virtual Work

	Technology	Work Environment	Processes	People
Readiness and Willingness	How effectively does the current information technology infrastructure support remote access and collaborative tools?	What is the attitude toward virtual work here? (Seen as mainstream, special circumstances, exception, or a perk?)	Which job families and functions are virtually conducive?	What are the management constraints? Supports? At what levels or divisions?
	Does the organization's budget support equipping and support remote team members?	How do the organization's culture and values support or contradict virtual work?	How do remote locations communicate and report to the rest of the organization?	What are the human resources constraints or supports?
	How does the organization handle equipment and network issues now?	Will virtual work have any impact on the customer?	How is productivity measured? How will that change virtually?	Overall, what do people like about virtual work or teams? Dislike?
	How might security policies need to change in an electronically connected environment?	Is the organization's core culture conducive to virtual work?	What systems are set up that support and measure virtual work?	How committed is the organization's leadership to virtual work as a strategic initiative?
	Is bandwidth adequate everywhere it will be needed?	What is the overall management style? Communication style? Meeting style?	What beliefs does your organization have about compensation and incentives? Do these change in a team or virtual environment?	What is the greatest challenge that a virtual team member faces? A virtual manager?
			Do reward systems recognize work across boundaries and collaboration?	

(continued)

Table 4.1 (continued)

	Technology	Work Environment	Processes	People
Readiness and Willingness	Is the mechanism in place for knowledge management access and sharing?	How are teams currently being used? How might that change if virtual teams are implemented?	How are employees career pathed? How will that change in a virtual environment?	
		Does the union support virtual work?	How well do current business processes support virtual work flows?	
		What is your competition doing with virtual work?	Are human resources, organization development, corporate communications, and other functions able to adjust their delivery mechanisms and policies or procedures to support virtual work?	
		How well designed is the office to accommodate more team meeting spaces? Drop-in cubicles?		
			How does training currently get done? How is that impacted by remote employees?	

(continued)

Table 4.1 (continued)

	Technology	Work Environment	Processes	People
Ability and Training Needs	Do the collaborative tools function in a way that supports business processes and people's needs?	What communication plans, educational campaigns, and other change management strategies need to be implemented?	Can delivery systems get resources and tools to the people when needed, regardless of location?	Do people know how to fully utilize collaborative software tools?
	Can data move quickly enough from workstation to workstation, regardless of location?	Are resources (time, facilities, budget) set aside for virtual team development and project planning activities?	Can training, product updates, and mentoring be delivered virtually, or in combination with face-to-face?	Can team leaders and members rally a team around a common purpose, and maintain commitment and productivity, regardless of dispersed team members?
	Do all have equal access to tools and training?			Are people trained in remote operations, netiquette and voicemail etiquette?
	Do team members know how to fully utilize the collaborative communication tools available, and are they comfortable sustaining relationships through tool usage?			
	Will any additional long-term support be needed?			

employees themselves. A simple, conversational interview guide is included in the appendix that can be used as is or adapted to better fit your organizational culture. Conduct this interview with key individuals such as executives, several or all middle managers, "functional" representatives, vendors, a few customers, and any others that seem relevant. Also conduct several group interviews, or focus groups, which represent every level and area of the organization. The results will yield rich data to corroborate and/or expand the findings of the original readiness self assessment.

Technology

International Data Corporation (IDC), a research firm, stated (2000) that U.S. companies are expected to spend $900 million annually on collaborative and knowledge management software, increasing to $4 billion annually by 2003. With such financial outlays, any responsible organization wants to spend their funds wisely. Knowing the answer to two basic questions will greatly increase your organization's "wisdom."

1. Will the primary focus of each tool be for pushing, posting, or pulling information only; or will it also be to build and maintain relationships?

Information tools are the easiest to implement, learn, and use. They are essential to a well-integrated knowledge management process, a learning-focused organization, and virtual teams. Knowledge sharing is a potent focus with rich potential for virtual relationship building.

Relationship tools have the most potential to really push your organization into a truly team-based virtual work world. Web conferencing and other groupware tools build trust, relationships, and interdependence among team members in ways that are—or soon will be—indispensable tools in any organization. An overview of knowledge management is explored more fully in a later chapter.

2. Is the tool to be a systemwide communication tool, or is it primarily for intrateam usage?

Organizationwide applications include functional and systemic "public" web sites, as well as internally accessed sites such as an orga-

nizationwide personnel directory, human resources policies and procedures and benefits information, the organization's strategic plan and
"state of the union" updates, electronic bulletin boards, and project
updates which impact the whole. They may be interactive as well, such
as a web cast downlink by the CEO to hold an all-hands live update.
These applications will usually be more "push and post" than team-
specific applications.

Team-specific applications are often more interactive, whether
information-driven or relationship-driven. Each team will have access
to the interactive databases and search engines, but will also usually
have a home team web site specific to its mission. Teams can have their
own list serves and chat rooms, document and resource sharing capabilities, and so on. The applications are available for the entire organization, but are utilized and customizable team by team or project by
project.

This section will identify the minimum technical tools needed for
virtual teamwork. A few guiding principles will assist your organization in making decisions which are sustainable and systemically sound.

- ✓ Groupware is not a political vehicle for reengineering your
  organization.

- ✓ Regardless of vendor promises, customization and learning are
  involved. Don't expect plug and play if you want the
  organization to get full value out of collaborative tools.

- ✓ Know your strategic goals for virtual work before buying the
  tools. Don't buy the tool first then try to find an application for
  it. Always keep customer, employee, and organizational needs
  front and center.

- ✓ Regardless of your short-term organizational commitment and
  capability to be a boundaryless and fully integrated
  environment, remember that is the direction your organization
  will go. Plan for increasingly interactive virtual teamwork.
  Keep future application intentions in mind when making
  current decisions.

- ✓ Don't just roll out groupware and expect people to learn it.
  Without training and reinforcement, they will use it as a
  personal organizer but few will ever see the wider applications.

✓ Expect and reinforce usage, but don't force the issue without education and training.

✓ Balance global rules and protocols for tool usage with the need of local teams to customize the protocols to support their unique needs.

Adding Virtuality — Workflow Tools

Before delineating the basic tools needed for virtual collaboration, two organizational issues have been typical in organizations that have been partially virtual. As this book suggests, groupware is intended to fundamentally expand the nature of how work gets done and how people relate with one another. In focusing specifically on organizational effectiveness in implementation of collaborative software like Lotus Notes and, more recently, Microsoft Outlook, two findings are particularly relevant as "lessons learned."

1. People's mental models about tools as a viable communication vehicle are the largest contributors to effective tool usage. If members view groupware as a necessary evil, a second choice, the tools will be approached warily, touched when required but not really embraced and integrated into "our way of doing business around here." Organizations need to lead the commitment to virtual tools by using them at the leadership level and throughout; by educating people as to their potential, benefits, and appropriate usage; and by training people in how to use them.

2. Organizational systems and structures that support, reinforce, and reward collaboration are more likely to achieve sustainable integration of the tools into people's daily behaviors. Without this, the tools will be used, but history suggests they will be used primarily as personal organizational tools. While this is helpful, this falls far short of the potential of groupware.

In summary of the approach to the collaborative tools, then, remember that the key focus is not on the tools themselves (many good ones are out there in the marketplace) but on using the tools to facilitate a culture of knowledge sharing, relationship building, and collaborative work. The virtual communication chapter will delineate even further the criteria to apply in deciding which applications work best for achieving certain objectives. With this in mind, let's look at specific tools, their purposes, and minimum requirements for a virtual team.

Intranets

Intranets and extranets are set up to enable and facilitate communication and knowledge transfer within a company. Some smaller firms don't need their own intranet; tools and resources available on the Internet can serve to create a virtual intranet. Most organizations have their own intranet and search engines. Minimally, the intranet should have online personnel directories and contact information, electronic bulletin boards, and web pages. A simple intranet might have a library or resource center. More and more organizations build a shared, interactive and fully searchable database. If knowledge management is in place in the organization, the library/resource center will be fully searchable and can become a very powerful tool.

Virtual teams can and should create their own web site on the intranet. This becomes "home base" for team members, stakeholders, clients, and other support or parallel functions. The web site can be as simple as posted information for updates and team member contact and availability information, although this doesn't capitalize on the site's potential. Virtual teams often have web pages for each team member that includes project or expertise specific information, as well as personal and other data. Often parts of the web site are accessible by stakeholders or clients.

Collaborative Groupware

Lotus Notes is the most well-known leader in this technology. Microsoft Outlook is also common, and there are many others available.[23] Collaborative groupware tools perform structured activities based on "rules" that govern document flow. Basically these tools make your documents smart. By setting parameters, or rules, the software

---

[23]I hesitate to list or endorse options because technology is changing so fast that they will most assuredly be different by the time this book is published.

will automatically mail a document to the designated person or group, including approval processes if desired. Only designees with approval power can check an approval box before sending the document on to the next person or group. Security rules are created to define who has access to what documents, who can modify documents, and who has authority to adopt permanent changes to a document.

Once the rules are set up, based on the infrastructure that the organization and/or team creates for tracking workflow, the team is ready to share documents, spreadsheets, and databases. Group calendaring and scheduling, email, group polls, listserves, electronic whiteboards, and chat rooms are common groupware features frequently used by virtual teams.

The disadvantage of collaborative groupware is that the designees may change, and the rules need to be modified in order to ensure that the work is flowing to the right people. This requires maintenance, especially if approvals or security is involved. Also, chat rooms seem not to have lived up to their reputation in a work context. While a great tool, some have found them less involving than hoped. Another disadvantage of chat rooms is that there isn't always a history of the chat, so any richness to the conversation may be lost.

Group scheduling and decision-making support systems such as polling features are probably the most utilized features of groupware. Even co-located teams let the computer take the headache out of scheduling and tallying.

Listserves

I'd like to mention a simple application that I have found underutilized. Grouped email appears to function much like a listserve, but is not as powerful a medium. By creating listserves for your team, or subgroups based on project parameters, not only do you keep everyone in the communication loop and involved, but you can easily poll or schedule. Even more importantly, however, is the threading that a listserve provides. With email, that critical message from three weeks ago sent by Jennifer about the client modifications can get lost in a folder. As a listserve, the email can be searched through the threads, and usually all attached documents and related postings can be called up as well. Yes, the threads can become overwhelming, but with thoughtful rules, this creates a history for the team that can be invaluable. A recipient can respond to the whole group just as easily. Any message posted, whether originated or as a response, is automatically distributed to the entire group.

If your organization does not have listserve capabilities, many Internet-based listserves are available, mostly free. Again, the industry is changing so fast that the available options will surely be different by the time this book is published. A couple that have been around for awhile, though, are egroups.com and powwow.com.

Instant Messaging and Chat Rooms

These are very popular in the larger population as a way to meet and greet people around the globe. They are used in very casual and social environments to cyber-date or to discuss "X-Files" episodes and everything in between. They are also an effective work tool. Synchronous online conversations can be very effective for many purposes, from asking for help to break through a mental log jam, to releasing some pent-up emotion at a critical point in a project. In a work context, I tend to think of them as hallway conversation or ad hoc confabs.

Electronic Whiteboards and Synchronous Conferencing

Video/audio/web conferencing is the ability to participate together live in a conference. A web conference can be screen-driven only, add voice, or add voice and video. Today video links are commonplace because the bandwidth is available, video streams have become fast and efficient, and the price point is very affordable. Several participants can all see and hear the same things at the same time. I can be sitting at my terminal in my home office, while you are sitting at a train station with your notebook logged into an Internet station. A facilitator can be conducting a live training event with us and several other team members. We are all seeing a PowerPoint presentation, brainstorming a marketing idea on an electronic whiteboard, and hearing (and possibly seeing) each other contribute.

With certain tools, the live (synchronous) session is being recorded while it is being conducted, so that it can then be posted in its entirety or in modularized mini-sessions to the intranet. That way anyone can participate in the session later—asynchronously. More interactive collaboration can occur without incurring high T&E. The project moves at a faster pace because the team is interacting same time, different place. This avoids unnecessary project creep that so easily occurs when Person A is waiting to hear back from Person B about Project Priority C. With conferencing capabilities, the right people can get pulled in right away. Again, watch the trade press, but two companies whose applications I have been impressed with are Interwise and Centra.

A major benefit of web conferencing is that it extends the possibility of affordable and timely participation in events. Before, it may not have been practical to fly everyone in for a project update, even though it would have been nice. With web conferencing, that changes. The ability to attend meetings and training is especially valued by people who, in a hierarchical company, would not be considered to be at a critical enough level to participate. Again, the tool serves not only communication, but to further develop the organization as an integrated web rather than a bureaucratic ladder of hierarchies.

But what if you don't have web conferencing capabilities? Not to worry. Audio conferencing with bridge calls is still a tried and true vehicle. The team can be bridged by phone and, depending on connectivity and tools available, still do synchronous document sharing and whiteboarding together.

Project Management Software
This has become practically indispensable for any team leader and team, regardless of work environment. In a virtual environment, it is essential as part of the workflow updating, feedback, and reporting process. Primarily managed by team managers and project leads, not much changes regarding its usage in a virtual environment.

Minimal Tool Training
Team members need to know how to search the Internet and organizational intranet effectively. Some may also need training on file and application translation, and the tools required to ensure that no matter what the format, a file can be read and modified accordingly. Group-

ware tool training is essential. Even those who know the basics, unless they have operated in a virtual environment previously, will not understand how to use the tools fully. Etiquette training can be built into the tool training through practice sessions. Chapter 6 details more fully how each tool is best applied and for what purpose.

Work Environment and Culture

Remember the key considerations regarding the work environment explored in Chapter 2. Most employees today are members of multiple teams but are forced to continue functioning in a silo environment. Organizations serve themselves when they structure themselves, their cultures, and their reward systems to support boundaryless relationships, networks, and collaboration rather than tribes, walls, and information hoarding. Furthermore, as more employees are offsite, they still come in occasionally for meetings and trainings. The physical workspace adjusts to support team and training spaces, as well as drop-in "hotelling" cubicles. Facilities take on a different look and feel, seeming more like a meeting place than an office. This is not to say everyone becomes a virtual employee, working off campus. It would suggest that many will, and facilities adapt as needed.

Business Processes

Following are guidelines to consider when redesigning systems and processes to better support virtual teams. Obviously not every system, process, or workflow has to be perfectly in sync with virtual work before an organization can get started. The virtual work organization readiness assessment provided in the appendix and summarized in Table 4.1 will help decision makers identify where the greatest supporting processes and obstacles are. Overall, build fairness into organizational practices. Use this as a guiding principle.

Job Definitions, Job Families, and Functions
- Work for cross-functional and cross-boundary, rather than core, competence. Management's role in job shaping becomes less about job descriptions and resource allocation, and more

about creating the integrated "web" of expertise, experience, and collaboration.

- Every job is expected to seek information and knowledge, not wait for it to come to you.

- When planning work teams, think competencies, not location or organization.

- Functional responsibilities and duties define one's expertise and competence, but do not limit access.

Some work is not amenable to virtual work without significant process reengineering, such as assembly lines, food service, and some on-the-job training. Other functions can become virtual but will require cultural and social, and sometimes technical paradigm shifts, like counseling, classroom "soft skill" training, and storefront retail.

Performance Accountability, Management, Measurement, and Control

Another chapter focuses on virtual management, but a few additional suggestions are relevant here.

- Remote performance management cannot be any more effective than current on-site management practices. Virtual work is an opportunity to look at current performance management practices and intentionally move to a more collaborative, shared responsibility approach to management by results.

- In a teaming environment, individual and team-based results, accountability, measurement, and rewards are required in order to sustain a team focus.

- More structure and planning are required. Management and team leaders need to become more planful, thoughtful, and organized.

- Less structure is also required. Command and control models of management don't work well virtually.

- Managers usually need some training in remote management. The good news is that many managers can use this as an opportunity to "brush up" on basic management and supervision, as well as expand their managerial competence in a virtual environment.

- With virtual management, poor managers usually show up, while good managers improve.

Rewards, Incentives, Success Sharing

- Change the reward system and measure people on their teamwork, sharing of information, and team results as well as or instead of individual contribution.

- Compensation should demonstrate valuing knowledge sharing and collaboration. Team-based and knowledge sharing pay/incentives are worth exploring. Generally, base a minimum of 20–30 percent of base pay on team performance. Please note, however, that the organization should do this only do if team members have high influence/impact on virtual work and team results. Warning: Large bonuses for being virtual workers send the wrong message that virtual team collaboration is above and beyond the call of duty.

- When results are achieved, find ways to broadcast the success so that team members are recognized for current success and future opportunity.

- Find ways to celebrate virtually and/or in person.

Career Management

- Human resources and virtual managers need to work together to assist individual team members' ability to exploit their position in the organization and to create opportunities and advantages for individuals and teams.

- Promote people for their competence, knowledge, and commitment to teamwork, and relationship and network management.

- Organizationally ensure and monitor that career opportunities are fairly distributed throughout the organization, regardless of work environment. If 75 percent of all promotions occur from the Chicago location, for example, and for few virtual workers, what message does that send about virtual work?

- Broadcast career opportunities electronically.

- Tie the organization's career management process tightly to the reward, recognition, and success sharing processes. Make them all interlinked and electronic as well as personal.

Knowledge Management

Again, a separate chapter addresses knowledge management issues. A few summary points:

- Learning is a social and cultural phenomenon above all. Whatever knowledge management tools are available, all should enable people to learn from themselves, people, and experience. Given this reality, learning happens through interaction with people and events. Therefore, once again the case is made that virtual workers need to be intimately connected to their work, their team, and their larger organization.

- As more organizations are at least partially virtual, the marriage of knowledge management and team collaboration becomes more critical.

Paper, Project, and Workflow

- Flow will vary from team to team depending on what the team's work is. Some high-level business processes will usually need to be adjusted to support virtuality. Obviously, paper and document flow should be as electronically driven as possible in order to keep courier and other delivery systems to a minimum, as well as to avoid unnecessary slow downs. In analyzing business process maps, identify what work is conducted simultaneously (parallel work) or serially (sequential work, such as in assembly line fashion). Also identify what work can be performed independently (does not need to be integrated with other work in a significant way) or interdependently (integration required, either simultaneously or sequentially).

- Independent parallel work or interdependent parallel work that doesn't need to be integrated except at certain junctures can be accommodated through simple groupware tools such as email, listserves, and other tools.

- Interdependent parallel work requiring constant or frequent integration needs to utilize groupware technologies such as chat rooms, virtual conferencing, document sharing with publisher and review protocols, and good old-fashioned in-person meetings.

- Sequential work. If the workflow passes from one or two sets of hands to the next, simple tools are adequate here as well. If many hands are handing off to many hands, distributed databases and document sharing with protocols, and virtual conferencing for the hand-offs are minimum requirements.

• Make sure the software fits your processes. Technological aids are just that—aids, not tyrants.

• Organizationally, published methods guide teams in how to implement its project management process in a virtual environment.

• In early phases of virtual teaming, have teams capture templates from current and previous work cycles. Use the knowledge management systems to perpetuate availability and usage of these templates. If not, the organization may be out of touch with the virtual team and can miss key lessons useful to other teams about how teams form, coordinate work, and disband.

• Protocols need to be determined to identify who has the authority and security access to draft and/or permanently change the team's work products.

• Whatever systems are developed, each should be capable of tracking and updating all previous versions of the team's work, including attached or related data.

• Any security, access, and usage protocols should be built into the flows created.

- Change flows to support virtual work, but no more than is absolutely necessary. Simplicity and easy integration with existing systems is always the overriding priority. Try not to add layers of bureaucracy; use tools already in play as much as possible.

Delivery Systems

Human Resources

Many HR departments are effectively utilizing their intranets to keep policies and procedures current and available to everyone, allow everyone access to their benefits package, educate employees about HR issues that impact them, and so on. These tools enable HR to fully support all employees regardless of virtual location.

Organization Development

Organization development functions are critical supports to virtual work and are significantly impacted themselves. They are usually at least co-responsible for successful implementation of change initiatives, and virtual work is no exception. The entire contents of this book are highly relevant to OD practitioners, including their need to examine how they currently deliver OD.

For example, if OD currently holds meetings (one-on-one, small group, and large group) on-site and in person, they will need to introduce virtual conferencing tools. If they collect data through surveys, focus groups, and interviews, then collaborative polling (anonymous and identified) and web conferencing tools are useful. The previous and next chapters have particular relevance for the OD function, which relies heavily on trust as a vehicle.

Corporate Communications

Like HR, corporate communications is usually quite adept at utilizing the intranet and Internet to fulfill its mission both inside and outside the organization. There is virtually no limit to the access points made available to a corporate communications department that is seeking a wide outreach.

Supply and Other Resources Delivery

Centralization of purchasing and other centralized functions make financial sense because of economies of scale and ability to harness and distribute resources efficiently. However, how does virtual work—especially if home-based or road warrior—impact such a simple delivery system as office supplies? If virtual workers are part-time virtual, the delivery system is not significantly impacted; people just pick up supplies while on-site. If they are mostly virtual, however, will that still work? Setting up master accounts with office supply stores, courier services, and other vehicles need to be decided in order for virtual workers to be as fully supported as their in-office counterparts.

Technical Maintenance

When all equipment was in one or a few locations, a maintenance program was easy. When equipment is literally all over the globe, different systems need to be created. Is a systemwide home-visit maintenance contract possible? Should equipment be leased rather than purchased, and maintenance built into the leasing agreement? Many options are possible, as long as the onus for maintenance is not put upon the virtual employee, expecting job duties to go beyond what is reasonable or fair.

Online and Call Center Support

Just because one becomes a virtual worker does not mean she should have to learn how to be a technical expert. Basic troubleshooting and maintenance makes sense, but what does the virtual worker do when basic strategies fail? Support should be available at all times team members may be working. If your organization employees are distributed globally, that may mean 24-hour support in order to follow the workday sun.

Other Virtual Work Support

Create a corps of "angels/helpers" who are experienced and committed to virtual teaming. These can be internal or external resources. They can help in areas as various as setting up a home office to managing the stress of the road to how to realign a troubled team. Use role modeling and virtual hand-holding for spreading groupware usage comfort. Create buddy systems to check in on virtual workers as they adjust to their new environments. Provide online and human access to virtual workers looking for specific advice.

Training and Development

You can't invest in technologies if you don't invest in people, especially in their training. Seventy-five percent of virtual workers and managers define company assistance and training as critical to virtual teaming's success. T&D delivery systems will increasingly become multimodal—some classroom, some virtual classroom, online, CBT, on-the-job, synchronous and asynchronous, and modularized. Despite technological capabilities, many trainers and learners are still most comfortable in a traditional classroom environment. Easing both trainers and learners into an integrated, multimodal delivery system is critical if virtual work is to become systemically sustainable.

When it makes sense, have the team members and manager participate in training together. Even if only a few of the team members are working remotely, the entire team is now a virtual team, so the training relates to all. Discussions and work sessions can then be practically applied to the group's team development planning process as it moves into a virtual environment.

Today everyone is familiar with Lotus Notes, Microsoft Outlook, and other like tools, but they may not fully understand the collaborative applications available. *Collaborative tools are **not** best learned in self-paced modules.* It may seem obvious, but I am compelled to ask, How is self-paced training a positive model for collaboration? Team training with meaningful demonstrations and chances to use the tools' capabilities significantly increases the likelihood that the tools will be fully utilized. Otherwise, the organization runs the risk of a powerful tool being underutilized, and a powerful team not fully reaching its potential.

In fact, one global professional firm found that its members were not beginning to tap the application potential of Lotus Notes to support collaborative work within their teams or with their clients. When they probed why, they found that they had not provided adequate training on the collaborative features, and people resisted using it except as a personal organization tool. They did little to integrate it into their team work practices. While they had been taught the mechanics of Notes, the training did not help users change the way they *thought* about workflow and working together using the groupware.

It is okay to deliver the training in a delivery method familiar to participants, or different modules using different methods, as long as the collaborative tool training is conducted such that the tools are actually *used*. If the familiar format is classroom, at least have some components of the tool training be simulated or, in fact, virtually delivered. If virtual workers are expected to conduct virtual web-based meetings using collaborative tools, for example, they must actually work with the tools during the training in as realistic an environment as possible.

Give people time to experiment and play with the new technology and provide real case exercises whenever possible (making doubly good use of trainees' time). If training exercises have real-world application, learning occurs while work gets done for the team. Otherwise, deadlines and other work pressures tend to take precedence, and voluntary "learning" either doesn't occur, or occurs when needed and under less than ideal emergency circumstances.

Once the organization is culturally conditioned for virtual work, some of the educational components of the learning objectives drop off, or are moved into new employee orientation programs, such as defining virtual work and why the organization is pursuing it. Some modules may only be relevant to telecommuters, such as setting up a safe virtual office. Following is a starter list of learning objectives to consider for a virtual work curriculum.

Learning Objectives for the Virtual Worker/Manager/Team
Organization
- Define virtual work and why the organization is pursuing it actively.
- Identify benefits to self, team, organization, and other stakeholders.
- Identify ongoing virtual work resources, supports, and next steps.

- Have a clear and shared understanding of virtual work policies and procedures.

Environment

- Adapt and thrive in a virtual work environment, regardless of work location.

- Assess workflows for feasibility and suitability of virtual work, adapting where needed and possible.

- Create and maintain a virtual "office."

- Create a safe virtual work environment.

Management

- Identify successful virtual worker characteristics and selection criteria.

- Identify appropriate use of various synchronous and asynchronous collaborative tools.

- Conduct and participate in virtual meetings and conferences utilizing various media and collaborative tools.

- Examine management methods that thrive in a virtual work environment.

- Identify specific vehicles for establishing swift trust within the virtual team and between the team members and virtual manager.

- Implement virtual performance management processes.

Creating Agreements

- Negotiate a virtual worker agreement.

- Negotiate performance standards, work and communication infrastructures, and protocols for the virtual team's functioning.

Skills and Competencies

- Increase technical competence with the various hardware and software tools.

- Understand and be able to implement basic technology troubleshooting steps.

- Identify appropriate use of various synchronous and asynchronous collaborative tools.

- Practice voicemail etiquette and "netiquette."

- Conduct and participate in virtual meetings and conferences utilizing various media and collaborative tools.

- Identify various virtual issues and determine solutions and strategies.

- Practice virtual work and prioritizing activities in a changing virtual environment.

- Identify specific vehicles for establishing swift trust within the virtual team and between the team members and virtual manager.

- Create pathways for virtual team member belonging, network development, knowledge sharing, and team synergy.

Remember that much real learning occurs outside the actual "training" environment. One of the best training tools is the buddy system. Partner experienced virtual workers with new folks, letting the experienced mentors provide just-in-time, practical, "real world" learning. This also encourages the values of a learning organization that gives forth rather than holding back, and models collaboration. This informal dialogue can be very rich, indeed. If the organization has a way to help capture this informal coaching, the entire organization benefits as well.

People

> We underestimated the technology needs. We corrected that the first year. However, our single biggest mistake was not understanding the people issues. If we were starting over we would spend more time and resources emphasizing training and communication.

So states Robert Egan, Director, Global Mobility and Virtual Work at IBM. The major focus of this book *is* on the people aspect of working virtually. As has been stated many times, technology is the enabler, but people are still the key. One additional point I will make here is this: *Whatever technology, systems, structures, processes, policies,* *procedures, training, or campaigns are developed for supporting virtual work and virtual teams, **all** should serve the needs of the people—* customers, employees, vendors, stakeholders, managers. People are and will always be the key to successful initiatives, and it is critical that any changes focus on making work *easier for the people.* If people have to do all the bending to fit a technology or a process, the initiative of virtual work will always remain an initiative. Sustainability comes from successful integration of technology, culture, and processes in service to the people.

Overall Organizational Rollout

It is one thing to connect terminals and to have common platforms; it is high leverage to integrate organizations. Integration changes the way organizations work, and the way people lead, follow, and cooperate. Communication **is as critical to the work as the work itself.** It is not a nice extra; it is the meat on the backbone of the integrated technology infrastructure. In order for integration to move beyond technical tools, organizations need to improve in these areas:

- Structuring themselves as interlinking and overlapping nodes in a web or network of teams and alliances, rather than as a hierarchical chain of command

- Encouraging and expecting frequent, full, and broad communication outreach, rather than following formal communication channel protocols

- Building a robust push, post, and pull knowledge sharing infrastructure, rather than static paper manuals and training programs

- Creating meaning at work for the many rather than the few

- Viewing people as a cadre of specialists available to the entire organization based on expertise, experience, and project/ team/client need, rather than a "member" of a certain department or function

- Thinking, dialoguing, and acting collaboratively together

- Pushing for learning and continuous improvement, rather than "cascading" information down and out from on high

- Mentoring and developing the next generation of leaders in multiple modalities, rather than "pairing up" based on function, geographic convenience, and politics

- Sharing responsibility for strategic direction setting and accomplishments, rather than delegating through the chains of command

Communicating with Other Stakeholders and the Larger Organization

Each team is part of a larger system and needs to connect back into the larger organization. In rolling out a virtual work initiative throughout the organization, education and communication is one of their four core elements. Any communication plan developed will vary from organization to organization based on culture, available communication vehicles and technologies, and other organization-specific parameters. Following is a composite of communication plan components and a generalized high-level example adapted from one client's virtual work initiative. This financial services industry client's culture is a highly hierarchical, bureaucratic control culture, and its experience with virtual work was minimal at the time. This particular team was a project team with organizationwide virtual work initiative responsibilities.

The Message   The message is the primary intention to be communicated to the larger organization. It is the basic building block in determining the rest of the communication plan. There are four key dimensions to the message component: What message is to be sent, to whom, via which vehicles, and at what time in the project.

The mission of this client, whom we'll call Financial Services, Inc. (FSI), for project Phase I was to allay fears and concerns, build understanding and commitment to, and generate interest in virtual work. Their message was, *"Virtual teaming is a viable workplace strategy, and an increasingly necessary strategy to remain competitive in a fast-paced, global marketplace."*

The secondary mission and message of the team was to scout the organization, gathering information on perception, readiness, willingness, and ability to begin or grow a virtual work initiative. The team would then leverage communication vehicles, among other initiatives, to "ready" the organization and create a sense of co-responsibility for virtual work's success at FSI. Their message was, *"Virtual teaming is a 'shared' responsibility among the organization, the manager, and the team members. We want to hear from you how to help you succeed."*

Target Audience   The team needs to think politically, influentially, and powerfully about internal public relations, relationship and alliance building and education/ambassadorial communication to build external commitment and understanding for the team's mission.

For the FSI virtual work project team, the initial overarching audience was the global credit business group. Within this group, there were four target groups: the division overall, the senior management group, the mid-level managers' group, and the line employees.

The team also needed to manage horizontal communication with related teams and functions, including information systems, knowledge management, facilities planning, and human resources. All these functions were represented on the team. Team members were the primary links to align activities, but the team elected not to rely exclusively on the liaison relationship for complete communication.

Vehicles   The teams needed to choose or create media, vehicles, and forums that were appropriate vehicles to get messages out and receive information back.

The FSI team elected to utilize communication channels that were already embedded in the organization: quarterly in-person town meetings with web casting uplinks to geographically dispersed locations, requisite monthly department meetings, the local public newspaper, the division newsletter, internal memos, broadcast email, and online discussion groups. These message channels represented select vehicles by which to send the information about virtual work. The meetings and broadcast email were also used to solicit information and feedback. Large "auditorium style" meetings were integrated into the town meetings, allowing everyone who was interested open access to information, to contribute opinions, and ask questions of the project team about the initiative and its status.

The message units embedded in each forum were customized to the target audiences. Each target audience received communications in at least four forums, such as a town meeting, a department meeting, division newsletter, and internal memos. That is, each target group received the message multiple times and differently, based on each audience's level of concern, amount of interest, and integrated responsibilities.

The team also developed a second-phase communication rollout that involved the creation and implementation of new communication vehicles:

- ✓ A web site was posted that included project updates and organizationwide personnel directories, including information about who was working on what aspects of the virtual work initiative.

- ✓ An electronic bulletin board was posted on the intranet and tied to the web site. The bulletin board had the added capacity of allowing anyone to post a question about how changes were being implemented, and to hear from others in the organization about what was occurring.

- ✓ An electronic suggestion box provided a way for anyone in the organization to make comments and provide ideas. The suggestion box could be anonymous.

- ✓ Once implementation began, virtual team members were sent frequent, even daily, updates about what was happening with virtual work, virtual work tips, and other organization updates.

When   From a project perspective, messages changed their focus depending on the project phase. The message structure moved loosely from the strategic to the tactical over the course of project implementation. As virtual work got underway, information became less educational/factual and more anecdotal to celebrate successes and provide tips.

Sample Specific Messages That Support the Overall "Message"
- ✓ FSI is committed for the long term.
- ✓ FSI trusts employees to do their job.

✓ Equity between traditional office and home office environments will be assured.

✓ Necessary job tools will be provided at remote offices.

✓ Ongoing training is available for immediate and continued success.

✓ Virtual work is a workplace strategy, not a right or a privilege.

✓ Systems will be adapted to accommodate career paths.

✓ Monitoring methods will be consistent with current performance evaluations.

✓ Virtual work may require some time in the traditional office, as negotiated between the manager and team.

✓ The manager will make it work.

✓ Enormous savings have been realized through virtual work (statistics cited).

Specific Scouting Questions Soliciting Input and Feedback

✓ How are we doing?

✓ What would make sense now?

✓ What have we forgotten to consider?

✓ What would make this easier?

✓ What barriers seem to be in the way?

✓ How are the managers doing in getting this underway?

Verifone, one of the most well-known virtual success stories, summarizes its systemic success in four core elements. These core elements can serve to guide the overall roll-out of virtual work in your organization.

1. Be eternally vigilant to build on success, remedy glitches, and support virtuality.

2. Constantly communicate at all levels of the organization.

3. Operate organizationally based on clear and unambiguous value statements.

4. Focus on ALL elements of success.

SECTION TWO

IMPLEMENTING VIRTUAL TEAMS

The barn has burned down!
Now at last I can enjoy
The sight of the moon.
—Tao

Three statements that are always untrue:
This is for your own good.
It's nothing personal.
As a matter of fact.
—Unknown

5

GETTING VIRTUAL TEAMS OFF ON THE RIGHT PATH

Coming together is beginning. Keeping together is progress. Working together is success.

—Henry Ford

The thing with high-tech is that you always end up using scissors.

—David Hockney

Andrea has been charged with implementing a fast-start project team to roll out fast. It is a great career opportunity, an exciting project with many people interested in participating, and she knows she can succeed with the right team. She knows what expertise, talent, and experience she needs and how to access the right people—she's been around awhile and knows her company, her network, and how to succeed. This team, however, must be a virtual one. While Andrea has participated on various virtual teams, both within her company and in other volunteer environments, she has never led a virtual team.

And she has questions:

- I know how to find the talent, but how will I know if they work well virtually?

- Are different competencies required to be an effective virtual team member?

- Are these competencies innate, can they be taught, and how much is a function of time?

- Should I consider individuals who have never participated on a virtual team before?

- How does my role as team leader change in a distributed work environment?

- How do I make sure we get this team started "right"?

- How do I keep the team aligned, focused, committed, and productive?

Perhaps you, too, have asked these and other questions. This chapter provides a fast-start, step-by-step template for getting your virtual team off the ground.

What Are the Critical Success Factors for Candidate Selection?

Jackson has been aching to work with Andrea for a long time, and this project is right up his alley in every way, including the virtual work environment. As a member of Andrea's project team, he could work from home. He approaches Andrea and, along with his other technical and expertise credentials, makes his pitch. He hates cubicles, prefers to be left alone to work without interruption, is self-motivated, and his only "black mark" is that he always arrives to work a little late though he stays as long as it takes to get the job done. To work from home would make getting to work on time a nonissue. He sounds ideal, right? Andrea thinks so, but she wants a tool to help her objectively review what type of individual tends to succeed in a virtual teaming environment.

There are no hard or fast "rules" stating whom will best succeed in a distributed work environment, but certain qualities and competencies have emerged as essential or highly desirable.

Essential Knowledge/Competencies
Communication Skills   Good communication skills are probably the most critical competency in a virtual environment. Much communica-

tion and feedback is written and by voice—both synchronous and asynchronous. Asynchronous communication is especially prone to misinterpretation and coldness. Clear articulation, interpersonal caring, effective listening, and clear writing are all essential in a virtual environment.

Job/Responsibility Competency   The first rule of effective team making, virtual or not, is to hire competent people in the first place. As a virtual team leader, you must have confidence that this person can do the job without continuous coaching or oversight. Trust in an individual's abilities allows the leader to focus on other priorities like team maintenance and project management. Many organizations stipulate that an employee cannot work in a virtual environment until they have performed their job responsibilities for a minimum number of months and maintain average or above average ratings on performance appraisals.

Technical Tool Competency   Ensure that all team members know how to use tools and have been versed in all hardware and software tools that will be required for communication and knowledge sharing. Team members must believe in, understand, and use the communication protocols. This does not mean that everyone must be able to tear down and reconstruct computers, or that help desks and other forms of support aren't available. It should not become an employee's "other job" to become a mini IT professional. Being trained in the basic tools, however, will save the remote manager, the virtual team, and others inordinate frustration.

Organizational and Time Management Skills   While these are valuable competencies in any environment, they are indispensable in a virtual environment, especially if the team member telecommutes part time or is a "road warrior." Setting up a virtual office, maintaining two or more work spaces, and coordinating communication and workflow requires a high level of organization and time management.

Desirable Knowledge/Competencies
Hardware and Software Troubleshooting Abilities   Basic training in how to troubleshoot common technology issues can save the company

money and the virtual team member time if simple solutions can be reached without on-site or carry-in technical support.

Problem-Solving and Independent Decision-Making Skills   One of the challenges of a remote work environment is that the next ready source for help isn't as simple as a holler over a cubicle wall or a quick call to tech support on the second floor. A second opinion may not be as readily available, and time deadlines may drive a need to decide without full input. If you are the kind of person who drives up to a full service gas station or asks everyone what they want for dinner before going to the grocery store, the autonomy and responsibilities of a solo office may not be for you.

Conflict Management   Willingness and ability to deal directly with opportunities, issues, challenges, and conflict are indispensable in a virtual environment where it is too easy to avoid issues until it is too late.

Knowledge of Company Policies, Procedures, and Cultural Norms   Even though virtual team members may not be in the corporate office every day, they are, nonetheless, members of an organization bigger than themselves and take on the rights and responsibilities of that membership. Knowing those rights and responsibilities, plus the informal "lay of the land," increases a sense of belonging as well as decreases the likelihood of unintentionally creating a risky or dangerous situation. This can be as simple and straightforward as being sure any external correspondence goes out on company letterhead with a common return address or knowing what phone number to give out for returning phone calls. It becomes quite confusing to a customer when two or three addresses, emails, or phone numbers are bandied about with a flip statement like, "Well, on Thursdays . . ."

Essential Characteristics and Qualities

Independent   Virtual employees must be able to work without the reassurance of others. Research indicates that the best virtual performers are those who can and who enjoy working alone, are action-oriented, and take initiative without waiting for permission. A philosophy of finding a way to make it work, and trusting oneself to find that way, carries virtual workers forward with confidence. Independence, however, does not imply an inability or unwillingness to work with others, especially in a team environment.

Interdependent, Especially if a Virtual Team and Not Just a Virtual Work Group   It's a myth that the independent virtual team member is any less committed to the team than co-located employees who see their teammates every day. In my work over the years, I've found many people believe that only introverts make good home-based workers. What I've found in reality, however, is that both extroverts and introverts succeed virtually, and, in fact, extroverts may have a slight edge because of their commitment to interaction and their willingness to create and maintain it.

In addition, just because someone works independently and virtually does not mean he or she operates in a vacuum. There are times when reaching out and seeking input, advice, information, or confirmation is required. Great virtual team members utilize resources when appropriate.

Resourceful and Innovative   One key to career success is often one's ability to build a personal network and learn how to creatively resource effectively. This is no less important in a virtual environment and becomes in some ways, in fact, even more critical to stay interdependently connected with the team and the organization.

Assertiveness   As much as an organization and a team leader attempt to keep remote members informed, usually the fear of "out of sight, out of mind" has some justification if not managed effectively by the virtual team member. The organization, remote manager, and team member all share responsibility for getting the virtual employee's needs met. Sometimes that means speaking up, asking for, or seeking out what one needs.

Able to Set Boundaries   It is not uncommon for the home-based virtual worker to become the neighborhood UPS and FedEx delivery stop. Until the members of the household and neighbors are "trained," family and friends may unwittingly assume that if someone is home, they are available. Telemarketers are also frequent interruptions. Household boundary management discussions and practice, separate telephone lines, set work hours, separate and sacred workspace, and other bound-ary aids help virtual workers stay productive and focused.

Simultaneously, virtual employees often need to set boundaries with work colleagues, customers, or managers. Disorganized or crisis-driven virtual managers or teammates can pull remote workers into the office more frequently than is really needed if the virtual team member isn't careful. Being available at all hours and all places is creeping into work consciousness today, which leads to burnout and work addiction. Everyone—virtual or not—has the right and responsibility to be unavailable sometimes.

Self-starter and Self-stopper   The previous characteristic focused on managing external boundaries. It is equally important to manage one's internal boundaries. In terms of starting work, being conscientious and goal driven increases significantly one's productivity. If you are the kind of person who has a hard time getting started in the morning, for exam-ple, creating some "getting-to-work" rituals may be very helpful. I once worked with a colleague who spent a lifetime in a highly structured work environment where the work routines predetermined his activities—the military and then a highly controlling bureaucratic corporation. When my colleague was suddenly thrust into a self-managing telecom-muting environment after nearly 30 years, he struggled until he hit on a routine that worked for him. He would walk out his front door in the morning, go to the sidewalk, turn right, and walk around the block. He would return to his house, walk in the door, and walk into his office. He was now at work. At the end of the day, he reversed the routine, returning "home." Sometimes a simple solution is all that is required.

What I have found, however, is not so much the starting work struggle, as the stopping work phenomenon. Virtual workers often stop distinguishing between work and home: "I just want to check email one more time before we watch that video." Two hours later . . . Work-weeks in the United States have slowly crept into the 50-hour a week range. Work addiction is at an all-time high. Technology has made ready access truly 24–7. If virtual workers aren't careful, they may find themselves "selling their souls to the company store" and not even rec-ognizing that they're doing it since work is so convenient.

Adaptable and Flexible   Another quality that is highly desirable regardless of work environment, a distributed work environment does have its challenges that require going with the flow. Networks go down. Technology malfunctions. Customer crises emerge. Plans and schedules change. Being able to anticipate, plan for, and flux with project issues and delays is a valuable quality. The more comfortable someone is with the unexpected, the more comfortable one will be in a virtual environment.

Reliable, Trustworthy, and Has Integrity   Doing what one says one will do is probably the biggest indicator of building trust among interdependent team members, which is critical to a virtual team's success. Meeting deadlines with little supervision is essential. This is discussed more fully in the chapter on trust and expanding emotional bandwidth.

Cooperative   Information sharing is power in an interdependent, collaborative environment, not information hoarding. Helping each other builds team commitment to one another and alleviates the risk of isolation and counterdependence of individuals.

Focused   Self-discipline and focus need to be internally derived rather than outwardly provided by the very structure of a "work place." The traditional office and co-located team habits externally assist employees to create focus on work. Outside the traditional environment, it is imperative that the virtual team member be able to create and maintain his or her own focus.

Desirable Characteristics and Qualities

Committed   Feeling a sense of "ownership" in a project and for the effective functioning of a virtual team yields a sense of belonging and responsibility. Being committed to stay the course and seek achievement for self and the whole helps individuals get past the isolation issues, which can be debilitating for some.

Service Orientation   In a virtual environment, it takes initiative and effort to offer and provide help. It's not as easy as hollering back a sentence or two answer over that cubicle wall. Understanding the importance of, and genuinely believing in the value of sharing knowledge, providing support, and desiring to help teammates dramatically increases the incentive to succeed in a virtual teaming environment.

Other Factors to Consider

Home Work Environment   Virtual team members are not all home-based, but for those who are, a separate and sacred work environment is essential. Making room on the corner of a dining room table is not conducive to a sustainable work focus. Virtual workers need a safe, ergonomically suited, well-ventilated, and lighted work environment. For a phone- and computer-based worker, that does not necessarily mean much space and could even be a corner in a spare bedroom. For other workers, it may mean a room set aside with desk space, computer terminal, filing cabinets, storage areas, and room for peripherals. What needs to be considered is how much space reasonably is needed, what safety requirements must be met, and can this space be removed enough from household traffic patterns to provide adequate work focus and sufficient home life separation.

Connectivity   Equipment requirements, telephony, and access speed issues will vary greatly depending on the job description. Minimally, most remote employees need to be able to log onto a network at 56K, and, for many, faster connection speeds are required. Further, most will need voice and data lines, whether through separate analog POTS (plain old telephone service) lines, DSL, ISDN, or cable modems. Virtual workers need to ensure that their virtual offices are located where telephony is not a barrier, and the domicile itself is electronically capable of increased demands.

With these criteria in mind, Andrea and Jackson are in a better position to assess Jackson's appropriateness as a virtual team member, whether some training and development might be required, if the work space can be accommodated, or if Jackson is not suited, for one reason or another, for virtual work. Again, there are no hard and fast rules, but some attention to these critical success factors can prevent many problems. Some success factors may be innate, but most can be taught and acquired with time and attention. Given commitment, job competency, and organizational support, almost anyone can become a virtual team member.

In the appendix, a sample virtual team member readiness assessment checklist provides a template from which to build a tailored assessment tool for your organization. This assessment tool can be used in a number of ways. It can be a self-assessment tool completed by employees who think they might be interested in a virtual work environment. Interested employees' managers can also complete it. If both the interested employee and the manager complete this checklist, they can sit together and discuss where they have shared and differing perceptions, and together assess suitability of virtual work for this candidate. The discussion can result in an action plan that includes preparations for remote work such as software training, telecommuter training, and home office retrofitting.

The Tao of Virtual Team Functioning: The Three-Fold Path

Chapters 3 and 6 address specific strategies for process maintenance to ensure high functioning virtual teams. Regardless of the tool kit, however, if every virtual team member and leader will commit to sharing responsibility for fulfilling three fundamental functions, virtual teams can create and maintain a smooth pathway.

Path One: Create a Cohesive Team Culture

Teamwork is fundamentally social. All groups with a common purpose need care and feeding. Virtual team members need special care. Despite becoming more commonplace, despite distributed employees being more accepted, despite organizations' strategic commitments to becoming truly global internally as well as externally, working as part of a collective that one seldom sees can feel isolating.

Chapter 3 discussed high- and low-context cultures. The specific ways of supporting the collective will vary depending on the cultural context of the group. Regardless, support is critical to team functioning in both environments. Simple team discussions should occur early in the team formation, and be revisited as often as needed to ensure continual collective well-being.

This is not to suggest that strict rules and regulations be created and stringently enforced, but it is important to decide as a group what kind of atmosphere you want to create and sustain. Teams can place priority on being personally supportive or work focused only. They can prioritize deep dialogue or not. They can be fast moving or reflective, risk-taking or conservative. They can exchange email jokes and cartoons or ban them as off limits. The nature of the team mission will drive some preferences, but the individuals on the team have a lot to say about the atmosphere itself.

As a team leader, think about what kind of mood you want to set for your team. What metaphors and symbols will you use to guide how people interact with one another? How will they think about their team purpose? A team is primarily social, and team members use that social relationship to get the work done. The atmosphere that gets created needs to support relationships, not just production. For example, a well-oiled machine is a common metaphor. Does that convey the essence of how you want your team to see itself? Is your team more organic, more fluid, like a koi pond? Is your team a web with many interlinkings or is it more of a road map with a clear direction and destination?

What styles, behaviors, and technical tools will support creating the atmosphere you want? What does interaction look like for your team? What role, if any, will power and politics play in this team, and between this team and the larger organization? How public does the group want to make its accomplishments? How involved will stakeholders be?

Again, there is no right answer, as long as the overriding focus is on individual and collective well-being. Whether this is a short-term, ad hoc project team or an ongoing team, there needs to be routinized scheduled time, whether virtual or face-to-face, for the team to come together for continuous rapport building, check-in and maintenance, and to make sure everybody remains aligned to the team's purpose.

Path Two: Support the Team Community

How many of us haven't had those days when we just aren't having a good one? The project is off track and behind schedule, the children are sick, the customer is cranky, you thought it was a casual day only to find out it was a client-on-premises-wear-your-business-best day, the network has gone down twice. These are the days when teammates become friends, when the extra support or cup of coffee is so appreciated. Now imagine having that same day in a home office. Network is still down, so no email whining allowed. Kids are running temperatures and can't be in school, so they are whining in the next room. You don't have to worry about the dress code, but the client is still cranky, making it difficult to juggle with the cranky kids.

Do you hate yourself for not downloading that big file to your hard drive so you could work without the network? Do you get so frustrated you call it a day and feel guilty for letting your teammates down? Do you bite your lip and muddle through as best you can, accomplishing little? Do you drive to a network dial in?

How do you spell relief? Do you call a virtual team member you've barely met in person and ask her to field the customer's calls today? Do you implement team-created protocols for expected challenges like technical access issues and dependent care surprises? Or do you simply call a colleague and blow some steam, enabling you to begin problem solving together and see more clearly again?

Yes. That's one of the functions of being a team, to support one another. Assuming professional integrity, it is not only acceptable, it should be expected that occasionally the team has to flex and help out. Part of creating community is taking the time before a crisis to develop relationships, to get to know one another, to identify together what attending to the well-being of one another looks like.

Interpersonal support doesn't have to be driven by personal crisis. Some people like to be more fully informed than others, while others prefer to have information on a need-to-know basis. It gets more complicated when one realizes that one person's need-to-know looks fundamentally different from another's. The potential negative results of not getting clear with one another about interpersonal needs and preferences are that of violating inclusion/exclusion issues and boundaries.

Marvin, for example, comes from a highly bureaucratic corporation where he learned to copy ten people on every correspondence, load every version of every document to the intranet, keep hard copies of every memo that ever crossed his desk, and ask his manager for "permission" about many things. Lorraine, Marvin's teammate, grew up professionally in a fast growth, entrepreneurial environment where one learned to act now, fix later. Marvin is a highly dedicated, competent, and creative guy. Lorraine is a highly dedicated, competent, and creative gal. Jack's modus operandi feels to Lorraine like information obesity, too much to bother with, and reeks of CYA behavior. Lorraine's MO is that unless her actions have an immediate or direct impact on a teammate's work, she will provide an update at the team's weekly conference call—in executive briefing fashion, very high level. Marvin likes documentation and tracking, Lorraine prefers oral reports with work production serving as the tracking device.

If both Marvin and Lorraine continue to operate in their preferred ways without discussing with one another or the team, how long do you expect there to be personal liking, knowing, trust, or respect between them? On rare occasions, that might occur. What seems more typical, however, is that Lorraine will begin to think of Marvin as verbose, a defensive bureaucrat or offensive braggart. Marvin will begin to think of Lorraine as a prima donna or loose cannon who has to be watched closely because there are few controls in place.

Loyalty and commitment to one another won't automatically happen in this relationship. Lorraine may even feel her boundaries are being violated when Marvin constantly asks to be kept "in the loop." Let's complicate the story even further. Lorraine works closely with Nell because their responsibilities are closely aligned and interdependent. Their work and their relationship are more fluidly interactive, so Lorraine naturally keeps Nell more fully informed. Marvin feels even more excluded. What begins as simple style differences and habits may develop into a perception of power and political game playing, intentional exclusion, and shortly, the focus of work becomes the interpersonal dynamics rather than the project or the customer. Place this in a virtual environment, and Marvin very likely may drop out and go unnoticed for too long before it is even noticed. In fact, if Marvin does overdo the email communications, his communication dearth may feel like relief rather than be noticed as an early warning sign of team dysfunction.

Most of us know that liking, loyalty, commitment, and willingness to participate with a group are desirable but not automatic. In order to avoid scenarios like Marvin and Lorraine's, decisions should be consensually made regarding issues such as the following:

✓ Who needs to participate in what decisions, actions, and commitments?

✓ Who needs to be included/informed/asked about what?

✓ What does participation with this team look like? Does it mean daily telephone contact with every team member? Does it include a sacred commitment to meet with the team in person monthly?

✓ How much information sharing is too much? Not enough?

✓ As a collective, what agreements can you make about pushing information and posting information, available for anyone to pull as needed or desired?

✓ When someone is struggling, what does "help" look like for this group? What is appropriate to ask, to offer, to leave private?

In other words, what does full support look like for this team? The rightness of the answer depends on organizational culture and norms to some degree, but, more importantly, the interpersonal needs and preferences of the team members themselves. Dialoguing up front can go a long way toward effective self-care for the team members.

Path Three: Produce Successful Outcomes

While collective and interpersonal support matters, mission accomplishment is still the goal, and all else serves this purpose. The trust developed within any team is fragile, and even more so in a virtual team if not reinforced by individual and collective performance that can be seen. It begins with a clear and shared purpose, vision of how that purpose will look when accomplished, and identified goals or outcomes to accomplish purpose. Every expert on team building stresses the importance of shared goals, vision, and purpose. With a true team (rather than a work group), add interdependency to achieve goals. An effective team achieves concrete, complete results—mission accomplishment, whether ongoing or with one final end result. Milestones and joint achievements provide the fuel to stay focused on mission accomplishment and the oil to lubricate trust.

In order to accomplish the mission in a virtual environment, more structure and planning are required. Emergency gatherings and on-the-fly planning are exhilarating and can be done virtually as the exception rather than the rule, but they cannot be the standard operating norm. Chaos and frustration results, and virtual team members see through the exhilaration to the disorganization lying beneath the surface.

If everybody starts with the same vision and knows what their Pole Star is, then even dispersed team members are more inclined to progress collectively. If there isn't an agreed-upon game plan and a clear structure for communication and feedback, it's easy for virtual members to work hard but get four degrees to the left of where the team originally meant to go. If it goes undetected, six or seven people are going in different directions without knowing it. What is more frustrating than working hard only to discover that rework is required because the focus was slightly off? Everyone needs to take an active role in making sure that all remain aligned to purpose.

Paradoxically, less structure is also required. Command and control management models do not work in a distributed work team environment. Trust is the glue holding production together, not controlling oversight. The mission and goals are for all team members to stay pointed in the same direction, not micromanagement.

As a group, discuss and decide the following questions together:

✓ What does task accomplishment look like?

✓ How "real" are deadlines?

✓ How does the group want to individually and collectively approach problem solving? Decision making?

✓ What authority levels need definition?

✓ Who has what project responsibility?

Virtual Team Formation

In order to succeed—on time, within budget, and without interpersonal fallout—all members are competent with the tools. Team members know their roles and responsibilities for project and team process success. They are aligned in terms of goals, team functioning, and project parameters. Like any good team, individual and collective strengths should be capitalized. The process by which the team agrees to operate should support team maintenance and integration of new or returning members. This section guides virtual teams through the steps to ensure success.

For those new to virtual teaming, virtual team managers need to transition teams systematically from their old co-located work style to the new distributed environment. Combine virtual and on-site collaboration early in the project. Increase virtual collaboration with team members' comfort and competence. If the team members have not typically worked on a virtual team, conduct initial meetings in person. Let the team know that this team will function virtually; define what a "virtual environment" is and what tools will be critical to the team's success. Train to the tools and reinforce their usage.

Move forward slowly until everyone is clearly committed to working virtually. Reassure team members that you, as team leader, will walk them through the process and any differences from a co-located environment; that they will have ongoing support (whether through the buddy–coaching model or some other support structure as people get comfortable with the environment); and that training is available (may be required).

Develop Virtual Tool Competence

Thanks to the increase in the capabilities and easy use of collaborative tools, virtual work has truly become as potentially and sometimes more vital a way of doing business as face-to-face interactions. The more competent teams are with collaborative tools, the more useful the tools become and the more efficient the team becomes. It used to be one could not get through a meeting without a whiteboard or flipchart, and then Power Point became the standard. Soon, collaborative software, online whiteboards, and web conferencing will be just as common a set of tools in every team leader's tool kit. Chapters 2 and 7 explore more fully when to use virtual tools and when to use traditional collaboration methods.

The must-have and nice-to-have tools will vary from team to team, organization to organization, project to project. Minimally, most teams' technical needs will include shared databases and documents, preferably synchronously interactive capabilities; project tracking capabilities; group scheduling and conferencing; email, instant messaging, and list-serves; and search engines. If your organization does not currently have these capabilities, all are available currently on the Internet, mostly free of charge, so this does not need to be a delimiter for virtual work. Again, a previous chapter explored these tools more fully.

Demonstrating, training, and providing practice with the tools can be done in a traditional classroom training environment, computer-based with wizards and self-study, or synchronously online. I have found the nervous majority is more comfortable in a classroom. Training tools are available today[24] that can video- and audiotape a live classroom training where participants are either on-site or online, while the technology captures the training synchronously for later replay or editing into asynchronous modules. It is important to begin the project with the tools that will be used throughout the project, and that any training actually uses the tools rather than simulations. Some tools are so user friendly that job aids and wizards may be adequate.

For reticent virtual team members, insist that the technology and communication protocols be followed. Coach, support, and guide, but do *not* let the expectations and standards slip. Reinforce increased use and competency. It is easy in the beginning to let resistance erode tool usage; *don't*. If a tool clearly is not performing well, or the medium choice seems inappropriate to the task, then—and then only—revisit the tool and make any adjustments or changes.

Ideally, this "readiness training" for a virtual environment will be organizationwide and will not fall to the virtual manager. However, most managers will need to provide some of this preparation. Once the members are competent with the tools, they are ready to develop as a team.

Virtual Team Roles and Functions
Traditional Roles, Representative Roles, and Virtual Team Support Roles   If someone has just been recruited onto a virtual team for the first time, how is his or her role different from working on a co-

---

[24]Check out www.interwise.com, www.centra.com, www.placeware.com, and other online learning tool and training companies.

located team? Managers need to help virtual teams identify roles and who (or how many) will be responsible for each role. All the traditional roles apply, depending on the team structure and organizational culture. If rotating leadership, for example, is standard operating procedure, rotation should continue in virtual teams. If it is a fixed and permanent team such as a work department, these traditional roles seem to fall out naturally.

Virtual team managers need to focus more intentionally on developing or delegating four virtual roles and corresponding responsibilities (which are often co-shared by all team members). Some responsibilities can and are filled by auxiliary or support team functions, and not individuals who serve on the team, such as technical support, training, and knowledge management specialists who help archive learning for the whole organization. Much responsibility, however, regardless of organizational support, will remain with the virtual manager and team.

Process Manager

All work groups manage the functioning of the group as well as the work, and this is even more critical in a virtual team. For all virtual teams and especially in organizations new to virtual work, spend time explicitly defining mutual expectations in a virtual environment. Since the communication behaviors and interaction dynamics are unfamiliar and often asynchronous and one way, it's easy to misunderstand, misperceive, and become frustrated with the virtual environment and with each other.

For example, let's return to Andrea's fast-start project team. Remember that Andrea is an experienced manager and project leader, but has not managed a virtual team before. Andrea typically holds weekly update meetings with a set agenda, including announcements. An announcement that might typically be made in a weekly staff meeting, if unclear or resisted by the rest of the team members, is obvious by members' nonverbal, if not verbal, response. The issue is discussed and/or clarified. Usually, if at all aware, the "announcer" can immediately tell how well received or understood a message is and can address it directly and immediately.

Now that Andrea will be leading a virtual team, she has to make some adjustments, including holding virtual meetings and moving some agenda items out of meetings and into other communication formats entirely. Announcements, for example, may now be delivered by email. What if that same unclear or resisted announcement previously handled in the weekly on-site team meeting were delivered to the team via email? There is no visual feedback, no immediate retort (at least not by the less impulsive team members) or, even worse, a "flaming" response by an impulsive team member could easily escalate into torte-retort, denigrating into missives rather than communication.

A verbal statement as simple as, "It is critical that everyone be at the product launch next Tuesday," when delivered in person with eye contact and voice tone, is readily accepted by all present. Take that same statement and put it in an email, and it can feel like an authoritarian command. This is true whether the statement originates from Andrea or a team member. All must attend to how communication affects the effective functioning of the group.

A team member in a traditional environment may or may not feel a sense of shared responsibility for the team's process and success, because there's a team leader and everyone is in the same place at the same time. There is an assumption that everyone will hear about what they need to hear about, will share what needs sharing, and it will just happen by virtue of the fact that everyone is in the same place. People don't have to be as actively making sure that they give and get information that they need. It's easier to let the co-located *environment* carry the burden for clarity and information sharing. In a *virtual* environment, unless **everyone** clearly takes full responsibility for full communication and feedback loops, it is easy to leave or be left out. In other words, every team member, regardless of other roles or responsibilities, is also a process manager. No one is off the hook.

The good news is, because it is a virtual environment, people take the process of maintaining healthy teams more seriously. Think about it. If you see each other every day, it's like a family who eats together every night. Because they dine together every night, they may think they know everything about what everybody else is doing, so they take it for granted and don't ask: "What did you do today? What's happening in your life? What did you learn? What do I need to know? How can we make each other's lives/work better?"

These days, we don't often sit down and eat together. When we do, it's more important to ask the questions, to stay informed. We're less inclined to take each other for granted. Virtual team communication and maintenance is, therefore, a blessing and a curse. The curse is virtual team members have to pay more attention to process, but the blessing is they take it more seriously and understand the value of it.

Communication breakdowns are usually unintentional. A significant percentage of company information and project updates occur naturally and accidentally by overhearing or being in the right place at the right time. Remove someone from the literal "water cooler" and it's surprisingly obvious how much communication occurs this way. And how much the virtual worker misses—unless intentional communication channels are created. I've been a virtual worker for a long time, so I know how it feels to be left out of the communication loop. And I know how it feels to be angry with that and to feel like someone let me down—my teammate, my manager, the human resources department, the account manager. In a virtual team, it's not going to do anyone any good to pout or point fingers. Everyone has to take a shared responsibility and feel co-responsible for making sure that no one is out of sight out of mind.

People in general, in a business environment, want to focus on the work. They want to focus on the content. Managing process is ignored or begrudgingly addressed when there is a problem, even though it is recognized as being as critical as the work. Teams don't need to go so far as to insist that everybody like each other, but there needs to be a balance. In a virtual work environment, people appreciate the balance and see the frustrating results when that balance isn't maintained, so they pay more attention.

Media Specialist

Every team member bears responsibility for understanding how to use the media and how to push, pull, and post knowledge. Also, in most organizations a support staff installs and maintains the media technology and trains and supports people in the use of the media. In addition, however, often someone within the team is responsible for ongoing setup, management, and facilitation of the collaborative tools. Who will arrange conference call bridges? Who will schedule and lead online conferences? Who will set up video feeds? Who functions as the liaison to IT and other media support when needed?

Knowledge Manager/Protocol Overseer

Organizations are increasingly committed to knowledge management, but until your organization has a fully integrated knowledge management system, the team will need to ensure processes for knowledge capture and sharing. Even then, some internal maintenance and protocol administration will be required. Who will manage your routines? Who will track various document versions and keep everyone focused on the correct document? How will audio conference notes be captured, stored, and retrieved? Who will provide thread protocols and train people in their usage? Is everyone responsible for maintaining the team web page? These responsibilities can be assigned, delegated among several, rotated based on logic, or remain with the team manager. How they are delegated is not as important as that clear responsibilities are planned before the team has unmanageable data that confuses and slows down the work.

Advocate

Whether virtual or not, team members themselves, *and their managers,* share responsibility for helping members along the career and opportunity paths. In a virtual environment, the team manager takes on some additional responsibility, especially when virtual teams are primarily project- rather than functionally driven. Team leaders should anticipate and design rotation schedules where appropriate. When a team project is ending or a team member's role on the team is ending, the team leader should work with the team member and the organization to create a successful transition into another meaningful project. Celebrating the team's accomplishments, ensuring that individual contributions are recognized within the team and in the larger organization, and helping to find another opportunity that will progress members' careers is an important part of advocacy.

Team Development and Planning Process

A team development process is a highly effective way to get a virtual team started right. If possible, bring the team together in person, especially if these are people who don't know each other or who are unfamiliar with virtual teaming. If it's not possible, plan and get acquainted virtually through listserves, chat rooms, and virtual conferences. With a team of virtual veterans, let the team decide the setting. I still like the idea of at least some face-to-face interaction, and the team development process is ideal. Include support functions and key stakeholders appropriately to build relationships as well as to build clarity about project expectations, communication infrastructure, and workflow.

Develop as few or many group process guidelines as the team desires, but commit to using them. Define common language, methodologies, and processes which all understand. Decide how to decide. Surface criteria for both project decisions and team process needs. Create and commit to the way the team will inform and involve one another and stakeholders. Aim for fair division of team care-taking labor. Agree also on not only what, when, and how information will be shared, but also on how team members will respond. Share responsibility for getting the team back on track if virtuality gets in the way. Meet support functions and people, and link with them as often and however needed. Make all in-person meetings strategic and relational, rather than informational.

Do things to create a sense of belongness. Post pictures of team members at workstations or as screen savers. Create metaphors and team anchors for all to use as their guiding connection and value drivers. Basically, attend vigilantly to the team's need to be connected to one another through both the work and the relationships.

The following agenda template outline can be used as is or adapted to fit your team and your culture. The more your organization works virtually, the more likely many guidelines will be standardized, or at least templated, simplifying the team development process, including making the team planning session more efficient. A complete team development process agenda checklist is included in the appendix as Sample Tool D. Each team manager merely customizes the complete checklist to fit her team's needs.

Session Agenda

I. Getting Acquainted

II. Team Charter, Vision, Values

III. Team/Project Planning (Project planning is the time for establishing project goals, identifying resources, setting milestones and deliverable deadlines, as well as delineating roles, responsibilities, and authority. This is also the time to decide how to share and embed learning, operating norms, and self-evaluation.)

IV. Team Process Planning (Process planning is the time for determining how to ensure that the team functions effectively together as a collective.)

V. Communication Infrastructure

VI. Membership and Maintenance

Virtual Team Maintenance

A successful team development planning process will serve the team well, but is not, in itself, enough. As frequently as seems appropriate, the team should review the norms and agreements, the systems and processes, and the protocols, and adjust to better fit the team and project's needs. As groupware tools are introduced, technical and user problems are common. Ask the team where the information exchange is working well or not working, what technical challenges are common to many/all, and what additional training or support is needed. Frequently revisit the communication infrastructure and its usage, effectiveness, and any modifications or recommitments needed.

Perpetuating Synergy

It's important to create ways for team members to experience membership. Some team members are used to being on teams and are good team players, but a move to a virtual team can be a bit jolting at first. If one is participating with a true team and the team interacts a lot, a natural synergy results. Part of this synergy is created by the energy built by being together in the same place at the same time. Synergy does happen with virtual teams as well, but it isn't the same as that extro-verted high. The team has to build that in, if it matters to them, through some other ways—virtual high-fives, conference calls, groupware, a more active use of email and other electronic communication, schedul-ing lunches with team members that are informal and celebratory, join-ing the same gym, whatever that needs to be. Schedule more social time than normally would occur in a co-located environment, even in a low-context culture team. This is discussed more completely in previous chapters.

The Rolling Present: Entry and Reentry

One of the benefits of virtual teams is that you can bring in new mem-bers from anywhere in the organization as required by the project, although the challenge remains in how to bring new or renewing mem-bers of a formed team up to speed quickly, especially if the team is mov-ing at a fast pace. This is not unique to virtual teams, but virtual teams do have a distinct advantage. Much work is done asynchronously and groupware helps provide a history, which can be sorted by time, topic, and other threads. On the other hand, the sheer volume can be over-whelming. The team manager needs to help new and renewing team members sort through the history for fast assimilation of knowledge. Questions to guide late-joining team members include:

- ✓ What reference documents, history, strategic planning documents, progress reports, and deliverables do joining team members need to review?
- ✓ Who do joining team members need to talk to, and about what?
- ✓ Who will serve as an orientation coach?
- ✓ How will new team members learn the operating norms of this team?
- ✓ How will new team members be introduced to the existing team?

The informal aspect of entry is more social. Minimally, virtual con-ferencing and other orientation strategies are necessary to introduce the new team member to the group and the group's culture, metaphors, routines, norms, infrastructure, and etiquette. Maintaining a team web page or electronic yearbook that includes social aspects are tools increasingly being used to electronically maintain team relationships and allow asynchronous orientation. They can never, however, fully replace the juicy human energy that gets created with live conversation.

In conclusion, a common myth is that distributed work leads to chaos. What is true is that consistent, integrated processes, delivery systems, and communication infrastructure will yield great results. Couple that with the full team's commitment to follow the three-fold path, and the course will be mostly smooth. The few rough spots will be recognized and remedied with little disturbance to the overall efficiency and high functioning of the virtual team. Following the roadmap provided in this chapter increases your team's success ratio significantly.

6

PRACTICAL GUIDELINES FOR VIRTUAL COMMUNICATION

The figure slowly climbed toward the summit of the mountain; hand over hand, pulling up toward the guru's cave. The climber reached the top, fingers raw and clothes tattered. He beheld the master: long white hair, wearing a flowing robe, indeterminate age. The master sat in the lotus position and seemed totally detached from worldly concerns.

The pilgrim knew he could ask only one question. A question for which there were no answers in the books, the journals, or from consultants. He approached the master and asked, "Master, what is the secret of virtual operations?" The master was quiet for a long time, considering this question. At last she spoke, "You could have sent email."

—*Ray Grenier,* The Grenierian Chronicles

Experience and research find that the use of electronic communication and collaborative tools significantly supports not only virtual work, but also virtual team members' identification with their organizations. Virtual work is supported or derailed often because of communication habits, patterns, and processes. A large obstacle is in trying to accomplish work using traditional communication methods such as person-to-person telephone calls and travel. In other words, the more virtual employees communicate and are communicated with virtually, the more emotional bandwidth is created among team members and between the team and the larger organization. This chapter explores communication guidelines, infrastructure, and standards for media and meeting forums.

Three major components need to be considered in choosing communication vehicles:

1. *Time.* Will the communication be same or different time (synchronous or asynchronous)? This chapter will explore both synchronous and asynchronous communication.

2. *Place.* Will the communication be in a co-located or distributed environment? Obviously, we will be focusing on a distributed environment.

3. *Medium/Forum.* If co-located, the group will be meeting face-to-face, and the forum is a conference room meeting. A meeting may be partially co-located with some team members conferencing in. If that's the case, the team room needs to be media-equipped for the remote connection. The remainder of this chapter will focus on media for distributed communication.

Obviously, technology has evolved nicely, providing many tools to achieve effective and timely virtual communication. They include forums such as the following:

- Instant messaging (alerts that pop up on a screen inviting an online "buddy" to chat)

- Private or group chat rooms (voice integrated or text only)

- Listserves (Mailing lists where messages are delivered to email boxes. Messages are threaded and often searchable.)

- Electronic white pages (online directories, often searchable by subject or interest as well as individual or group)

- Electronic whiteboards (for writing or sketching together during online collaboration)

- Group scheduling (using collaborative software to schedule meetings and seek multiple members' availability)

- Electronic bulletin boards (for posting messages that can be retrieved by all interested)

- Decision-making support systems (anonymous and named voting, polling, and other nominal group technique decision-making tools)

- Document sharing (Multiple users can access and modify the same files synchronously or asynchronously.)

- Web conferencing (using collaborative software to meet synchronously or asynchronously)

- Videoconferencing and video streaming, web casting, or audio conferencing (People are in multiple locations, usually participating at the same time. Some tools "record" sessions for later replay or modularized use by asynchronous participants.)

- Voicemail and email

General Principles for Selecting Forum/Media

Many people associate technology—particularly computer technology—with storing and exchanging data. This is discussed specifically in the knowledge management chapter. Although knowledge archiving is a critical success factor for virtual work, never forget that communication is the most critical success factor for any enterprise, virtual or not. Virtual leaders have a responsibility to model and teach communication using virtual media and forums. No one choice will always be the best choice, and the more competence in multiple tools, the better.

What are you trying to accomplish? Match the medium and forum to the intention of the communication. Remember what you have learned about the importance of sacred virtual space. Medium, forum, and people all contribute to the setting of that space. How people interact—how deeply, thoroughly, honestly, thoughtfully, quickly, slowly, patiently, individually, or collectively—is greatly influenced by medium, forum, and who else is in the "space." For example, a telephone conference call with three or four people can be highly interactive, fast paced, energizing, and as productive as a face-to-face meeting, assuming there is no need for visual focus. Take those same three or four people and place them on a facilitated bridge call with 100 others, and the telephone conference takes on a whole different feel. The medium is still the same—the telephone. The forum, however, has changed from a small virtual meeting to a facilitated event with rules for participation, such as muted telephones. There will be a clear leader/facilitator to "guide" the meeting. A bridge call is usually a one-way feed with some limited interaction component, such as a motivational speaker or a CEO "state of the union" address with Q/A at the end.

By the end of this chapter you will realize what wide choices are available. Simple questions will guide team members and team leaders in effectively matching media/forum with the intention, or communication goal. The overriding goal is always, regardless of medium or forum, to support the three-fold path:

- Create and sustain a cohesive team culture.
- Support the team community.
- Produce successful outcomes.

Overall, let these questions guide:

✓ *"What is the intention of this communication/meeting?"*

✓ *"Do I have any limitations to consider?"* Is there a time or cost factor that might limit choices? A participant comfort or competence consideration?

✓ *"Who is the target audience?"* Is the target a team member or two? The team manager? An intact private team? A customer? The entire organization? Anyone interested?

✓ *"What is the focus of this communication?"* Is it primarily information sharing? Relationship building and interaction?"

✓ *"How critical is time?"* Is immediate communication required? Is an immediate response equally as critical?

✓ *"What tone do I want to set?"* Is it to be formal or informal? Personal? Strictly professional? Warm or neutral? Fast or slow pace? High or low interaction?

✓ *"Is a certain sense of space and presence more appropriate?"*
What space and "presence" will match the tone, focus and
intention of the communication?

Let me say more about space and presence. For example, in co-
located work environments, much "real work" gets done in very casual
environments, like bathrooms and break rooms. You may set up two
or three open and ongoing chat rooms or listserves for different types
of work communication. One may be called "The Virtual Water
Cooler" or "The Break Room." Other work gets done casually by
walking by cubicles, happening into conversations, and "oh-by-the-
way's." What forum is available for posting and participating informally in conversation and a sort of appropriate "work gossip"? Perhaps this forum could be called "Walk-by Shoutings" or "Tips and
Taps" where people can share tips and tap the wisdom of the collective.

I am a member of one conference planning team that communicates
through multiple media, including potluck dinners every few months
(we travel some distance to be together); individual side conversations
(telephone and email); a listserve called "The Virtual Hot Tub" for more
casual, free flowing conversation and planning logistics; and another
listserve named for our specific purpose of online dialogue. This second
listserve is content and mission focused. Each team member initiates
communication in the forum appropriate to the communication. When
someone initiates a private interaction with another individual using
either listserve, the group gently reminds her or him of how invasive it
feels to receive emails that have no relevant content to the rest of the
team. The caring and commitment of the team to the collective comes
through in all forums, yet each forum has its own "presence" and tone.

When audio and video are added, this changes the "space and presence" yet again. It is not just "more." Being heard and/or seen changes
the sense of presence. If a team has video cameras on their desktops, for
example, team members can scan their workspace, giving others a "picture" of the environment their teammate works in each day. Having a
face or voice to go with the words, whether live or in our mind's eye or
memory when the words are text or email, "warms up" the conversation. Aural and visual clues hold value and meaning long after the
interaction is complete.

Sometimes the team leader may want to experiment with various media and forums for variety, and to notice the differences in team dynamics. The more choice that a team has, the more competence in multiple tools, the more flexible and powerful the team is.

Overall, as we become increasingly competent with virtual tools, the limits of application are less. If your team is relatively new to virtual communication and collaboration, a general guideline might be that virtual media and forums are ideal for eliciting divergent opinions, especially when combined with anonymous decision-making support systems like polling. Virtual communication and meetings are highly effective for knowledge and information sharing. Virtual tools are also good for getting a "pulse" of the team regarding how divergent or convergent their thinking is on a particular issue. If time is limited, consensus is needed, and difference of opinion is great, a team unused to the virtual tools may be better served by meeting in person to reach consensus.

As team members gain tool competence and high trust in one another, even complex and conflict-ridden issues can be resolved with virtual communication. The group's communication habits, norms, and culture (high or low context) are a greater influence on media and forum choice than the tool per se. There is no hard or fast rule of thumb beyond assessing the group's readiness to tackle complexity in a virtual environment. Suggested uses, inappropriate usage, and advantages for various media follow. Always, let purpose, priority, and desired meeting tone be your guide.

Email

Email is a destination address where an individual can be reached virtually, regardless of geographic address. It is great for quick, short messaging that keeps conversation, project pieces, and information moving. It is good for straightforward and noncontroversial communication, fast review of documents using file attachments, and logistical coordination if collaborative software isn't available. It has also become a great stress reducer and relationship builder via jokes, inspirational stories, and other messages. Each team and organization needs to set its own ground rules regarding non–work-specific messages.

Email is best suited for one-on-one communication and occasional group messaging and copying others in. That and telephone communication are probably the two most common one-on-one communication tools. In fact, it has become an indispensable mailbox address for almost everyone—in some cases more important than a postal address.

It is not good if the sender is expecting fast turnaround, especially if all teammates are not online all the time. The subject line is critical for sorting the type of message, but even with that, emails can pile up quickly and become difficult to sort through. All email packages have storage and organization capabilities, and most have automatic sorting functions, but many fast-moving people don't stay on top of their virtual filing cabinets. It is *not* the place (in most cultures) for high emotion and interpersonal difficulties to be managed.

Also, as with all communication tools that are one-way with no immediate feedback mechanism (beyond notification when a message has been opened), it is easy for misunderstandings to occur. Without the added clues of voice, eye contact, and body language, a message can be "heard" much differently than intended. For example, one virtual manager found that problem communication styles between two team members were magnified when the workers began to rely primarily on emails. Therefore, the manager insisted that for those particular individuals, the first communication attempt had to be by telephone. This was not "normal protocol" for the team, but it demonstrated situational leadership in order to accommodate the negative impact of remote communication on this particular relationship. It eliminated the problem. No virtual team should rely solely on one-way communication vehicles such as email to get work done or maintain relationships.

Broadcast Email and Listserves
This is a better vehicle for group communication. It's great for announcements and any communication that impacts more than two people. Listserves have all the advantages of email with the added feature of threading. Threading tracks the messages sent so that they can be sorted and tracked in various ways, such as sender, topic, date, or new postings since the reader last logged on. The advantages of this are obvious: new or missing members can get up to speed by reviewing the history, "lost" messages can be searched more easily than they can with email, and the tool does some of the organizing for the team. Listserves also usually give the member a choice of having messages automatically

delivered to her email address, or be held on the server until accessed. Like email, however, the lack of immediate feedback from this one-way message increases the likelihood of misunderstood meaning.

Live Voice

The telephone and voice-over-Internet is still an indispensable tool for two-person conversation, as well as small group conference calling and bridge call conferencing. The gain in immediate, live conversation is a much richer, more accurate communication than text-only forums like email and listserves. With wireless and all the forwarding options today, it also increases significantly the likelihood of getting a person needed now, not later. Obviously, it is great for highly interactive, immediate, fast movement and conversation. The disadvantage is the lack of a record of the conversation to refer back to if needed. Outcomes and actions taken because of the call are dependent on individual memory and any notes taken.

Voicemail and Pagers

Occasionally people are still not available, and voicemail becomes a great tool for relaying a complicated message, a more sensitive or emotional message than one would prefer to communicate with text only, and at times when you don't want to disturb the receiver, such as during a teammate's off hours. It is a one-way medium, however, and holds the disadvantage of that. It is not a good medium for long messages, anything involving a need for the listener to digest much information, or resolving conflict.

Audio (Telephone) Conferencing and Bridge (Telephone) Calls

Conference calling is a great way to hold meetings if a visual focus, like a shared document, isn't required. It's also helpful when holding a face-to-face meeting if one or two participants can't make it, but can attend virtually. Conference calling is good for high interaction with small groups. Bridge calls are better for larger groups when a presenter or speaker is the primary focus, with questions and answer periods built in. When participating in a conference call, remember to identify yourself by name each time you speak; you want people to focus on your message, not figuring out who is doing the talking.

Chat Rooms

People seem to either love or hate chats. Some insist that the artificial environment interferes with full conversation, while others love it as a medium for work, online community, and other forums. Increasingly, providers of chat rooms have voice options as well, which speeds up conversation for the keyboard impaired! Keep chats to a relatively small group, and remember that any group member can lurk (watch without participating), so a chat is not a truly private conversation. Instant messaging is a better choice for dyadic, private conversation.

Instant Messaging

Instant messaging is just like a chat room, except it is between two people and you don't need to go into a chat room first. Through an ICQ (Internet Chat Query), a team member can seek another team member to see if he is online at the time. The IM chat box pops on the screen, and you're live! Many wireless phones are now also capable of instant messaging, so team members can still be reached by IM even when away from the computer.

Electronic Bulletin Boards and Team Home Web Site

The bulletin boards and web site serve as a team tool, as well as a bridge to the larger networked organization. Post and store upcoming events, what's new, hot links, team personal web pages, documents and information, and whatever seems relevant. Many intranets have the capability to have a team web site with security measures. Firewalls allow certain audiences in to certain parts of the site, while the team can have access to the full site. A customer, for example, can access a "storefront" and product delivery schedule, but not be able to access living documents that are not deliverables yet.

When a team member wants to get a quick overview of where the team and the project are, this will be the first stop. When a new team member joins the group, this is a vital forum for orientation.

Video Conferencing and Web Casting/Streaming Technologies

Video is no longer a high-end solution. It does not mean, however, that every virtual team should insist on it. If video can add something to the meeting or conference, then add it. For many recipients, however, data is still being moved through 56K modems, and, even with streaming technologies, the throughput can slow down the transmission. With asynchronous playback, that may not be an issue; the document, animation, or presenter's image can be buffered and stored in temporary memory. If the conference is live, however, bandwidth still matters for many.

A video conference is still an option, especially if you have a team distributed regionally and you want to send an important message to everyone involved in a project, or even the entire company. It can be set up as one-way or full feedback, depending on the meeting's needs and the budget. Web casting and video conferencing are more cost effective if the audience is large. With web casting, some limited interactivity is usually possible, such as polling. It is a perfect forum for large "keynote" meetings like CEO State of the Union addresses, keynote speakers at web (or in person) conferences that will have wide appeal, or any time a team needs to send a consistent message to a large audience. What is also nice about streaming audio/video/large documents is that team members don't need to store huge documents to their hard drive.

Web Conferencing

Web conferencing is similar to web casting, but it is more interactive, depending more on the collaborative software tools. It is economical for small or large groups. Web conferencing can occur synchronously or asynchronously. Most web conferencing software is designed for trainings or conferences and meetings, and includes decision-making support systems using nominal group techniques like polling, group scheduling, document sharing, electronic whiteboards, a personal notes section (how nice to take notes without interfering with anyone else), and chats. Many also are developing streaming capabilities with video recording capabilities. For synchronous web conferencing, most tools have feedback features for the facilitator, such as speed up, slow down, and so on. Chat rooms run simultaneously in corners of the screen. A Q & A box is available where participants can post questions or take the floor, and some software lets the facilitator turn over the "reins" and let others "drive" the meeting.

Many still find web conferencing cumbersome in a team meeting format because there are built in limits to multiple simultaneous input. While this ensures organization to the meeting, sometimes organized "chaos" is necessary to get juices going for synergy. Sometimes people just talk all over each other in meetings, and that can be a good thing. Some software now gives the facilitator the option to "open the mike" to the entire group at once, providing more flexibility. This can still be confusing if everyone tries to speak at once. I have learned how much people rely on visual cues to know when to "jump into" a conversation. Without the visual, it's easy to accidentally jump in and "step on toes." A combination of voice and visual (web conferencing collaborative tools) increases effectiveness tremendously.

Facilitation of a web conference is similar to face-to-face or audio conference facilitation, but there are some virtual facilitation competencies worth noting. In person facilitators often rely heavily on their observation skills and personal charisma. These elements—especially if video is unavailable—are missing in a web environment. The feedback features are intended to replace observation, but they are limited in effectiveness by how willing meeting participants are to share their feedback.

The facilitator also has to be comfortable driving the tools. This isn't difficult, but a little practice goes a long way. For newcomers to web conferencing, pick a fun and low-stress meeting topic to start so that people can focus on increasing tool competence and not the content of the meeting per se. And, of course, basic training for all, especially the facilitator, is very important.

Participants also participate slightly differently. I have found that they tend to be more aware of what they say and how they say it because it is "captured and recorded." This is great in a high-trust group because the group can improve what someone puts "out there" so it doesn't have to be perfect—following the tenets of good brainstorming. On the other hand, participants are also more self-conscious about what they say because it becomes part of the record. If two weeks forward a district manager wants to know "Who made that reference to X?" the record makes it possible to *know* who said what. That's great for tracking and accountability, not so great for anonymity and hiding behind the group, unless the opinions were specifically solicited via anonymous polling.

Another nice feature of web conferencing is that the group can work on multiple ideas by turning to multiple whiteboards. The team can sustain many conversations in separate "places" without being chaotic. This is easier when the conference is asynchronous, but can work synchronously as well, as with breakout groups with individual assignments. Different facilitators can be assigned to guide the conversation for every breakout topic.

As with most collaborative tools, the captured data simplifies orientation of new or returning team members. It is important, however, to facilitate a good summary of each session. What were the key learnings? What were the key findings? What decisions were made? What are the next steps? Just because there is a literal history of the meeting doesn't mean a good summary should not be captured. Most team members do not want to have to refer back to a conference unless they have a specific need. Good facilitation always includes helping the group "ground" their learning and outcomes before parting ways.

Synchronous Web Conferencing   Synchronous, or live web conferencing acquires more energy and enthusiasm that feeds on itself. Everyone, or almost everyone, is present NOW, and this supports fast movement. An advantage of synchronous web conferencing is that meetings are generally shorter, and the time forces the team to prioritize and focus time and attention. Having a facilitator helps this prioritization, focus, and energy building also. Sideline conversations (sidebar chats, for example) can occur without disrupting the meeting flow. Decisions and work are recorded and captured, making next steps easier. The shared documentation and whiteboarding (similar to a flipchart) serves to keep the team focused and ensure that all have a shared understanding of what was said and decided, since everyone is walking away with the same documents. One disadvantage of synchronous web conferencing is that extroverts may overrun the meeting. It's also easier for quiet members to remain quiet. Facilitators need to be aware of this.

Asynchronous Web Conferencing   Asynchronous web conferences can have one subject or entire "learning tracks" with different events scheduled at different times. Synchronous web presentations can occur and be captured for asynchronous participation. Team members can "attend" the whole conference or only those sections relevant to their responsibilities or interest. Time becomes a range rather than an event.

People have a chance to prepare (no excuses not to), think, leave and return, and do research during their "session" without disrupting or slowing down others. Side conversations cannot interrupt the meeting. People can start at different times. More thought can go into contributions. Teammates can step back in and continue to contribute based on additional input from other teammates since the last "visit" to the meeting space.

If facilitated and focused well, web conferencing, synchronous or not, can serve to unite a team around a specific goal or learning, just as effectively as a team rally. It becomes a working tool, a learning tool, a knowledge management tool, and a team-bonding tool. Who can argue with that?

A communication goal or intention may not be able to be fully accomplished through one forum. For example, Andrea is responsible for her fast-start new project that has several parameters and customer requirements that are set. She wants her team to come to the initial planning session with this knowledge, so she posts this information on a bulletin board on the team's home page. Because of the relatively new virtual environment and the fast turnaround and fluid nature of the project, she schedules a two-day on-site team development planning session. Even though every team member is physically present in the team room, she uses collaborative software so that decisions made and materials created can be organized immediately for everyone's access. The physical "presence" is important, however, for the group's culture and need to consensually decide together. Multiple other meetings and communications will occur as the project gets underway, exclusively through virtual communication tools like synchronous web conferencing for project updates, instant messaging between team members, document sharing, and so on.

As virtual managers try different possibilities, they may not always be happy with the results, especially in the beginning. When technology is used and it doesn't seem to work, it doesn't mean the virtual tool has failed. It could be just a bad meeting, a lack of practice or competence, the meeting design, the facilitation, or the tool itself. Examine all possibilities before giving up the tool.

One last point about virtual communication is a reminder that facilitation of virtual communication is not only done in a fixed time and space. The team manager facilitates communication before, during, and after scheduled contacts and meetings. It takes time to learn how to read the cues regarding how well people are communicating through various media. Be patient with the learning curve, and "check in" more frequently and actively about the perceived quality of communication until the team feels competent in each tool and confident in the team's ability to track their group dynamics. Do this formally at the end of every meeting or milestone, as well as informally.

Team-Specific Communication Infrastructure and Communication Standards

One key accomplishment of the team development planning session is the creation of a communication infrastructure. Creating the basic infrastructure takes some real team thinking. How will updates be done? What information needs to be passed on? What decisions should involve everyone? It's a simple set of questions, but it's critical in a virtual environment, and it can go a long way to ensure that rapport and trust don't break down due to unintentional misunderstanding, and that everybody has clear mission and team alignment.

The team needs to agree on a strategy to manage and coordinate communication. A warning: This can become too cumbersome to be useful, so choose as few processes as possible for exchanging critical information. Communication should be:

- Standardized
- Organized
- Timely
- Easy

Table 6.1 Virtual Communication Infrastructure

Who	Needs to Talk to/ Respond to Whom	About What	For What Purpose	Through What Medium/ Forum	In What Time Frame	How Often	Who Else Needs to Be Informed
Manager							
Team							
Individual Team Members							
Strategic Partners							
Customers							
Support Functions							
Other Teams							
Other Stakeholders							

Make a commitment to honoring the agreements, modifying agreements and protocols as needed and as agreed to by the whole team based on experience or changing need. (See Table 6.1.)

One of the hidden dangers always lurking on the sidelines of virtual teams is the ethic that everyone needs to be involved in everything. You can avoid this recipe for disaster by clarifying which tasks need everyone's input and which do not. On the other hand, when in doubt, err on the side of overcommunication. Communicate often, even if nothing is pressing. If there is any question, decide based on maintaining the network and relationships. Create a schedule of activities to keep people involved and informed. Create obvious feedback loops to ensure that communication keeps moving.

Protocol Guidelines

- Contact information and availability

- Have a team home page that has a virtual availability board: who's at work, offline, on vacation, working but not available, and so on

- Have each team member maintain a personal web page that contains:

  - Full contact information

  - Professional expertise, qualifications, and experience

  - Primary project roles and responsibilities

  - Technical limitations (e.g., Someone has only one dial-up connection so cannot be online and on the phone simultaneously.)

  - Preferred media contact (e.g., email first, voicemail second, wireless third)

  - Typical check-in frequency and response time for various media (if not set by team protocol)

  - Time zone, work hours, and off-hour availability

  - Other team-defined personal information

Email, Listserve, and Voicemail

- Decide who should receive copies of emails (cc's) or who an email should be forwarded to for what types of messages.

- If distribution list should be blind (addresses not revealed for privacy) or open (posted so anyone can access any email address from the distribution list).

- Use subject lines as a flag, indicator, and sorter.

- Decide daily and off-hours commitments to check in (e.g., 4 times daily during core work days, 1 time daily during weekends).

- Set length limitations.

- Create topic guidelines.

- Decide participation requirements and acceptable response times.

- Decide what is urgent and how to prioritize messages sent.

- Decide appropriate and inappropriate uses for each. (e.g., Listserves are not used for one-on-one or subgroup conversations. Email is not used to confront another team member regarding an interpersonal conflict. Internet jokes and other humor are/are not acceptable.)

- Agree to tone, acceptance of colloquialisms, and other "marginal" communication styles.

Rolling Present

Unless clear protocols are set for "checking in" not only to voicemail, but to the team web page, shared documents, and other work products, there may be disparity among team members about what is considered "current." What is considered "current" is usually driven by how much time has passed since a team member last logged on. A team member with DSL may be logged on up to 24 hours a day, and he may check his team home page and email several times a day. For him, the current is literally backlogged only by hours. Another team member may be on dial-up with a 56K modem and only one phone line. She may also be committed to multiple teams and this team's project isn't her only priority. She may only log on once daily. For her, the current is about a day. If you have several members who update too frequently, it puts stress on everyone else because things go too fast. You may need to set and adjust protocols to slow down or speed up the pace. This is also dependent, of course, on the project demands.

Project and Commitments Update and Workspace/Workflow Management

Without clear protocols for how to organize the workspace and documentation, things can get confusing, especially when team members are sharing documents. Workspace input and information can be organized many ways, as needed by the team, customer, or organizational protocol. Minimally, input should be searchable by time, subject, and person responsible. Separate areas can be set up for different project pieces, individuals or subgroups, or whatever makes sense.

A teamwide space for tracking and review is also helpful. Here anyone can check the schedule, review past work, follow the project progress, or check on others' project status to see what is upcoming and eliminate redundancy. This becomes a project and team management tool as well. It also enables joining team members to get up to speed quickly. While this may not appear to be a "communication" tool in the purest sense, try working as a virtual team without it, and see what unnecessary communication occurs from pure frustration!

Documentation and Storage Guidelines

These guidelines and team-defined protocols will also eliminate much confusion:

- Create and work from predefined templates for plans, reporting mechanisms, status updates, delineation of customer requirements, change orders, cost estimates, and any other relevant documents. As everyone gets used to the templates, they are easier to work with, read, scan, and interpret.

- Create a tracking mechanism for document revisions, availability and usage by whom, and authoring and authority guidelines for recommended revisions and accepted revisions.

- Put page numbers, version numbers, and dates on all documents.

- Decide acceptable applications and software/versions.

- Decide the work storage space(s) for complete and current documents, information that is no longer useful, and deliverables.

- Develop security protocols.

- Develop metrics and accountabilities for how well the team complies with protocols as well as deliverables.

A healthy caution is necessary here. Databases can become quite cumbersome if not careful. Information obesity is a real danger for virtual teams because people tend to overreport as a strategy to feel connected and noticed. This is especially true if trust is mediocre or there isn't much interaction among team members or between the member and the manager. Overreporting is a way to make sure that everyone "knows how hard I'm working."

Information obesity can also occur if the document storage protocols have no mechanism for sorting and weeding information that has served its purpose. Just because we *can* store lots of information doesn't mean we *should*. Individual members may have different preferences, and may want to "store more" information than others if they choose, but on a personal folder. For example, remember Marvin, the bureaucrat, who likes to overinform? He may want to packrat every version of every document, and he *can*, but not on the team's space. Lorraine, the fast-moving teammate of Marvin's, may have the opposite challenge. She may, based on team protocol, need to document more than she would otherwise. The negotiated protocol is to be committed to by everyone. As a team, decide what and when to archive information.

Whatever happens to paper? The prognosticators used to say we were fast moving to a paperless society. It hasn't happened yet. It probably won't. Paper is comfortable and easier on the eyes. What is important to virtual teams, however, is that work is *moved* electronically instead of with paper.

Communicating Learnings

A real risk of distributed teams is losing the accidental learnings and sharings that more naturally occur in a co-located environment. When teammates see one another's work, listen to their struggle, spontaneously pitch in on a stuck point, wander into an insight during a casual conversation on the way to the break room—amazing insights, patterns, and breakthroughs can occur. If distributed teams have a weak communication infrastructure, the synergistic discovery is less likely to happen. Emergent knowledge not only needs to have opportunity through synergistic cooperation and communication, it also has to have a way to be communicated with the "whole," whether the whole is the team or the larger organization.

Gestalt psychology declares that the whole is greater than the sum of its parts. A team should be more "intelligent" collectively than any individual is alone. That is the power of teams. If the communication infrastructure doesn't support cooperative discovery, learning, and communication of learning, it is not functioning to its full capacity. Therefore, any communication infrastructure should include intentional dialogue, deeper conversation, and informal chatting so that the forums can evoke new learning.

When new learnings, insights, or information is valuable to the whole (again, team or the larger organization), the communication infrastructure should have a strategy to "push" the information out to people. If it is relevant but not critical, the infrastructure may have the option to "post" the information for people to access when they want or need it, rather than forcing the data on people.

Virtual Meeting Management

Virtual meetings can be a very powerful time- and cost-savings tool. A major telecommunications company in Denver held a two-hour meeting with 11 people. They documented a financial savings of $8,000 by holding the meeting virtually. With the reality of today's global marketplace, even nonvirtual work environments need to hold meetings virtually.

Virtual meetings have their own energy. They move differently than most traditional meetings. Because of the collaborative tools, they are used to *accomplish* work *as the team discusses* the work. Documents can be created and modified on the spot. In general, meetings are shorter. People get weary in most meetings if too much time passes, but in virtual environments more focus is needed visually (if using collaborative tools), aurally, kinesthetically (keyboarding), and mentally. If the meeting is to be a working session, limit the number of participants so that everyone can fully participate, and limit the subjects covered. As a facilitator, aim for shorter, more frequent meetings with work and dialogue continuing in between.

Meeting Protocols

- Create symbols for various types of meetings that are included in meeting announcements. It helps team members prepare for the meeting. For example, brainstorming sessions could be symbolized by a lightbulb.

- If the team works in multiple time zones, rotate synchronous meetings based on time zone.

- Identify who can call a meeting, determine forum and media, and facilitate.

- Determine protocol for scheduling and responding to a request for a meeting.

- If the meeting is an audio conference or bridge call, those not speaking should mute the telephone.

- Agendas are set and sent out in advance.

- Prework is identified and completed prior to meeting.

- Meeting summary notes or products are synthesized and available after the meeting is complete.

- Summarize decisions and outcomes before debriefing the meeting.

- Each synchronous meeting includes time for process debrief before the meeting adjourns.

- Decide attendance requirements and options for each type of meeting. For example, update meetings are attended 80 percent of the time and can be attended by conference call or in person. If asynchronous, attendance time frames and response/actions expected are identified.

- Be a little early or on time. End on time.

- If not obvious, identify self as prelude to comment every time. This is especially important if the meeting is an audio conference.

- Create some method for ensuring that all participants have an opportunity to participate, including soliciting input from silent members.

Meeting Preparation

Virtual meeting preparation, whether synchronous or asynchronous, requires a little extra preparation. This responsibility can be solely that of one person, or shared among the caller of the meeting (usually also the facilitator), the process manager (if one has been identified), and the media specialist.

Based on criteria discussed earlier in this chapter, the caller of the meeting (facilitator) must select the appropriate media and forum for interaction, including a decision about synchronicity or asynchronicity. The facilitator must determine who should participate and how to inform those impacted but unable to participate. The meeting is scheduled, and agenda and background information are distributed.

Prior to the meeting, the media specialist must ensure the following:

- All participants are competent in the technology.
- The technology has been reserved (if applicable), set up, and tested.
- Connections are working.
- Any security measures have been taken.
- Participants have the information, platform, and access codes they need.
- Any other logistical support has been anticipated and provided.

Starting the Meeting

If the meeting is asynchronous, textual or recorded background information is critical to give participants a sense of place. Include such items as who will be participating, what the time frame for completion is, what previous and next steps occurred/will occur, why the meeting is happening, and guidelines/expectations for how to proceed. This will be especially helpful for new virtual teams who are still adjusting to the environment.

For synchronous meetings, introductions and some ice breaking conversation is very helpful to help all participants connect to the group. The simplest way is to cycle through participants with something like the participant's name, where located, and what the weather is like. Acknowledge who is not present in the "virtual room" and what plans have been made for informing missing team members. Often people begin to arrive in virtual space over a several minute period. Casual conversation should be facilitated as everyone waits for staggering joiners.

Facilitating the Meeting

Depending on your technology, meeting participants' visual focus will be a PowerPoint presentation that is web cast, a shared document, or an electronic bulletin board. People are used to being visually focused, so be especially sensitive to the need for this, even if the group isn't actively working on a product. The visual focus between meetings also helps the group feel like a team. Rely more heavily on images and metaphors to help "ground" the team into the project and each other. Refer to symbols, pictures, graphs and charts, analogies, or whatever helps the group "see" or "hear" the same thing.

Note that when web conferencing, two primary threads of communication are occurring simultaneously—the visual focus on the screen and the conversation(s). While as a species humans multitask fairly well, one focus always takes priority. It may change several times during a session, but one focus will reign. In a virtual meeting this is obvious. Sometimes the visual focus is the anchor for the meeting, and conversation revolves around whatever is on the screen. (This is similar to a presenter relying heavily on his PowerPoint slides to guide the seminar.) Other times, the visual focus will be forgotten, or will be used as a tool to support the conversation. The conversation may be in chat or oral. A good virtual facilitator can sense where the "power" focus is and works with that energy.

Many teams meet in a variety of forums, including face-to-face. If your team meets both virtually and face-to-face, recognize that most people will have a preference. Since many team members are still most experienced with face-to-face meeting interaction, don't be surprised when that forum is preferred. Mix it up if it's practical, but don't let comfort zones keep people too stuck in the past.

Closing the Meeting and Continuing the Connection

As everyone who works with groups knows, the meeting ends but the communication and collaboration do not. The facilitator anticipates, encourages, and intentionally creates pathways for continuing discussion and collaboration for an appropriate period after the official meeting ends. This facilitated continuing conversation is especially relevant in virtual teams in order to keep everyone from "going to their own corners" and feeling like they've just gotten a bunch of work to do that they are now on their own to complete.

Communication is the backbone of all collaborative work, virtual or not. Synchronous or not. Technologically supported or not. Attend to it. Get better at it. Enjoy the synergy that results.

SECTION THREE

MANAGING VIRTUALITY

Old habits are strong and jealous.
—Dorothea Brande

To die for the revolution is a one-shot deal; to live for the revolution means taking on the more difficult commitment of changing our day-to-day life patterns.
—Frances M. Beal

7

VIRTUAL MANAGEMENT

What Are the Critical Success Factors for Remote Management?

The digital universe is a portal to connect people with people . . . The technology is the clothing on the actor of this interactive space experience.

—Jaren Lanier, Lead Scientist, NTII

Jared is the virtual manager of a long-standing team that moved to a virtual environment six months ago. Three of Jared's five team members are telecommuters, and each moved to a home office at least four months ago. He is not himself telecommuting, but the team is now truly virtual. All team members work in the office one day every other week, spending a bulk of the day in a teaming room together, reserving a couple hours for team members to network, scout, and schedule other meetings.

Jared and the team love the new arrangement. All received training and support from the organization. The team participated in a team development planning process in order to create and adapt the systems and structures needed to support a virtual environment.

In the last month, however, Jared has noticed a few things that are causing some concern. Janet has been lukewarm to his friendly phone calls and in-office conversation. He has clearly demonstrated concern for her welfare, but is a little confused about why she hasn't opened up about her struggle. Her performance has been declining rapidly for about three weeks. Janet has been a virtual worker for four months.

Mark, on the other hand, is setting personal records. His performance has been consistently improving over the six months he has been telecommuting, and he is beating deadlines on occasion. Jared's communication with him has been focused on making sure that he is aware of his responsibilities and expected standards of performance. Jared is pleased with Mark's performance because, frankly, he was the one team member for whom Jared had concern. While a bright and competent team member, he sometimes needed a little extra prodding to stay on schedule. Jared was worried that the lack of structure that came with virtual work would make him even less reliable and harder to manage.

Mavin, usually able to take initiative and responsibility, is not responding well to the team's recent redefinition of standards in a virtual work environment. Mavin is still in the office and does not want to telecommute, although she is supportive of the others and willing to participate on a virtual team. She seems to especially struggle with document protocols and some of the communication infrastructure commitments. She relies heavily on telephone communication, even when the infrastructure that the team agreed to designates alternate media. This has only recently come to Jared's attention.

Don has also remained in the office for the time being, but hopes to begin working from home within two months. He's waiting for the school year to start so that he can have fewer distractions as he finds his "telecommuting rhythm." Jared has noticed no struggle for him thus far with virtual work.

Chang began telecommuting six months ago and is probably the most transparent virtual worker on the team. His transition has been so smooth, in fact, that Jared has to remind himself to check in since he has so few needs.

Recent reports from two project team members indicate that interpersonal difficulties are occurring among team members. The team has a great success record and has accomplished goals over the long term, both as a virtual team and an in-office team. All are well qualified for the current project, and all are committed to the virtual work environment and the team. Jared doesn't know much about the interpersonal difficulties, but knows something needs to shift. He personally has noticed that Janet isn't contributing as much during face-to-face team meetings, especially when Mark is the meeting lead. Mark is an aggressive self-starter who has always been a motivating spark for the team, even though he isn't a strong finisher. Jared isn't sure why Janet is resisting Mark now when she never has before.

Jared is not overly concerned because he has worked with this team for two years. He has watched them work through issues before, and it has generally yielded a more committed team and a better service delivery to the customer. In fact, he is grateful that he has this team. At the same time, Jared knows that the virtual environment is new and requires his active facilitation.

Poof! You're a Virtual Manager

If even one of your team members is a virtual team member, you are a virtual manager. Whether you are a virtual employee yourself or not, you are managing remotely. Virtual managers are an important part of a virtual team's success. Organizations find that the attitude and managerial style of the virtual manager and upper managers are equally as important to successful virtual work as those of the virtual workers themselves. The difference between traditional management and virtual management is subtle, but significant.

There are some critical aspects of a virtual team manager's role that must shift in order to support her team in a virtual organization. No longer is co-located the ideal and distributed team members the compromise. High-level interaction, interdependence, and performance can occur in multiple work environments, and it is up to the manager to take the lead in effectively managing the full spectrum of virtual teaming for high performance. As Mary Francis Jones, formerly of Lifeway Christian Resources states, "We have found that managers who are willing to reevaluate the way that work gets done are much more likely to be successful and have successful teleworkers in the new work environment than those who just want to continue to operate as if the old processes were to continue and just have telework layered on top."

Although the collaborative technology gets much attention when discussing virtual work, it's really the changes in the flow of teams that creates new challenges for virtual managers. Virtual teams usually meet virtually *and* face-to-face, and work independently *and* interdependently. Managing a virtual team means managing multiple environments and workflow processes in ways that support the virtual team and its members. This chapter assists the virtual manager in managing the transition from a co-located to remote environment, facilitating team productivity and results, and facilitating organizational connection in a virtual environment.

Managing virtually means designing and managing a network of interdependencies, creating and sustaining many relationships, and all the while keeping the team focused on mission accomplishment. It is active management, focused on connection, communication, and performance. Virtual managers need to be excellent communicators through multiple media—written and oral communication and facilitation skills are a must. Regardless of organizational excellence with virtuality, virtual managers are still the primary link between their teams and the organization and strategic vision. In a virtual environment, this is even truer.

Virtual Team Member Development Stages

Managing a virtual team requires no magic pill. It does require being more planful, thoughtful and organized, clear in communication and coaching, and sometimes more intuitive about the team and team members' challenges and satisfactions. As team members adjust to a virtual environment, managers will need to facilitate their team's successful movement to full productivity as quickly as possible.

Typically, virtual workers will go through four stages of development (see Table 7.1). The manager's coaching will be around developing virtual worker competence in the new virtual environment: new and adjusted work habits and workflows, structures and processes, and, if appropriate, setting up a virtual office that fits the virtual team's infrastructure. It is important to note that the manager is not coaching around job competence; that is assumed and remains unquestioned. The adjustment to the virtual environment is the focus. Otherwise the virtual worker may conclude that the manager no longer trusts people to remain high performers. Janet and Mavin are probably in the second stage of virtual worker adjustment. Janet's struggle is behavioralized

Table 7.1 Adjustment Stages and Virtual Managerial Responses for Virtual Work Environment

Virtual Worker Adjustment Stage	Effective Virtual Manager Response
Stage 1: Let me start! Little experience in a virtual environment but much enthusiasm to work virtually is most characteristic of this stage.	**Response 1: Clear Instruction** The manager provides practical assistance and maintains close contact regarding the virtual worker's performance and development of virtual work habits. Little emotional support is needed since the virtual worker is already excited!
Stage 2: Bummer! Some healthy virtual work habits are beginning to form, but the frustrations and challenges of any significant change are front and center. Some people may want to quit, including the virtual manager.	**Response 2: Reassurance** The manager continues to provide practical guidance to the virtual worker. In addition, the manager reassures the virtual worker and provides emotional support. "This too shall pass." Don't give in to the urge to pull out. Back up a step if necessary, but don't quit. Support may take the form of advocating in the organization to provide additional/improved resources and organizational support.
Stage 3: I don't know . . . Solid virtual competence is developing, but the emotional frustration still looms large in the virtual worker's consciousness.	**Response 3: Reality Check** The virtual worker is experiencing some insecurity, but solid "virtual job competence" is developing. Provide less practical guidance regarding the actual logistics of the virtual environment, and more accurate feedback to help the team member see the good that is developing. Help the team members increase their self-confidence by noticing what is working.
Stage 4: Yes! Systems and processes are in place and working. The virtual worker is cruising!	**Response 4: Delegation** The virtual worker is working independently and interdependently, so the manager provides coaching only when the virtual worker elicits input or other indicators are evident. The manager will need to provide significantly less emotional support.

through withdrawal, and at this point, Jared's assessment is a hunch. He hasn't verified what her withdrawal is about. As a good manager, he will obviously explore the root cause before jumping to solution.

Jared scheduled a meeting with Janet the next time the team comes in. If Jared is right and Janet is in the second stage, then providing mere support will not be enough. She needs support *and* specific coaching regarding how to meet performance goals *in the virtual environment.* Jared knows Janet can do the work, but he is not convinced she knows how to stay involved with the team when working virtually. The coaching session would focus on root cause analysis, clarity about the need for performance to remain viable, and how Jared could assist her in getting back on track.

Jared's hunch was that Janet was facing isolation issues. What he found was something else entirely, but more on that in a minute.

Mavin, on the other hand, isn't withdrawn at all. In fact, she is calling everyone all the time. Again, assuming some adjustment struggle typical of the second stage, a coaching session is appropriate, focusing on support and guidance. With Mavin, Jared discovered two things. She has elected to stay in the office because she knows she likes the social component of an office as well as the structure. Oddly enough, even though Mavin remains in the office, *she* is the one facing isolation issues. *She misses seeing her teammates every day!* Because she is so committed to her team, however, and because she knows how much the telecommuting team members want to be home-based, she feels guilty for wishing things were "as they were before." Here's a great opportunity for Jared to help Mavin adjust to the environment and redefine what "connection and community" looks like for this team.

Interestingly, Jared's second discovery from his coaching session with Mavin was to discover that Mavin wasn't reaching out to the team virtually in order to stay connected with her team community except by telephone. She attended the technical tool training, but she acknowledged that she isn't comfortable with several of the tools. Because of her discomfort, she relies on the telephone.

A little further digging gave Jared a very important piece of information. Everyone values Mavin, and no one wants to call her on her protocol violations, so up to this point, everyone has been accommodating her without confrontation. Jared, because he works side by side with Mavin, hadn't realized this was happening.

The easy fix here is to help Mavin increase her tool competence and comfort, especially ICQ and instant messaging. The result—honoring the protocols, thereby respecting the team, eliminating low-grade resentment by others, and increasing Mavin's sense of "real" connection with her teammates. A simple training issue, recognized quickly, resolved many possible simmering problems.

Mark's issue was a little harder to recognize, and the impact on the team was Jared's only clue that there was a problem. Mark is a performance angel, a dream come true. He thrives in a virtual environment and has actually shown career potential that Jared had never seen before. So what's the problem? He *is* thriving in the environment, and he is loving it. Unfortunately, however, Mark knows that he has traditionally been the team member that Jared monitored a little more closely, and with good reason. Mark, bless his soul, is so busy trying to *prove* that Jared's faith placed in him is well deserved, that he has put stress on the rest of the team with his enthusiasm and excessive productivity.

Jared's job with Mark is to back off the guidance and reminders about standards, provide feedback about how well he is doing, and reassure him about how Jared has noticed his remarkable ability to perform well in the virtual environment. Jared hasn't said anything yet, but he's thinking that he may, in fact, make Mark a "virtual buddy" for Janet.

More on that in a moment as well. . . .

Team Development Stages

Just as individual team members go through adjustment stages, so will the team. This will be so whether this is an existing team that is moving to a virtual environment or a newly formed team that begins in a virtual environment. Much is written about the stages of team development, so we won't traverse that ground here. What is important to recognize, however, is how a virtual team's development is different.

Assuming some level of focus on developing and sustaining swift trust, virtual teams don't always go through the same predictable stages of team development, and, if they do, they do so more quickly. Despite the virtual manager's best intentions, however, often a team will hit a wall before fully settling in, as Jared has discovered. This may take the form of collective frustration at the perceived lack of organizational support or inclusion, interpersonal conflict on the team, task or role confusion, feelings of isolation, or some other obstacle. Good planning, an observant "virtual eye," and swift intervention help the team break through the wall and quickly settle in to high performance that is sustainable.

Jared's virtual eye and swift intervention, for example, revealed an interesting development that was easily managed because it was caught early. Mark's desire to prove himself was looking good at first glance, but it was subtly and negatively impacting the team. Mark's natural enthusiasm had gotten out of balance, and this was putting stress on the team due to the interdependent nature of their work. Janet was feeling the largest impact, and her way of coping was to simply withdraw. Jared's best intention to have Mark be a virtual buddy for Janet was the catalyst that broke the conflict wide open. Inadvertently, Jared's solution worsened the problem, but it also exposed the issue, allowing the team to work out a solution together.

The team openly discussed the pressure, which to that point had been more of an uncomfortable gnawing feeling more than a clear team understanding of the problem. Mark acknowledged his unconscious desire to prove himself, and how he was pushing himself, and therefore, the team too hard. Janet admitted that she personally liked Mark so much that she didn't know how to articulate her frustration, especially when all his ideas were such great ones. The team agreed to capture all the creativity, then prioritize and focus on what made the most sense in the time frames available. Jared watched as the team hit a new creative high, and the synergy created carried over into exciting synchronous and asynchronous collaboration for days afterward.

In developing and sustaining swift trust, it is the virtual manager's charge to facilitate the team's planning and development, including creating systems, processes, and infrastructures as discussed in previous chapters. Managing will include helping the team make the inevitable and necessary adjustments to ensure that the original "plans" adapt as needed. If the system isn't working, adjust the system. For many, the transition to virtual management is a big one that requires some testing and improving. Expect adjustments; see the strength of flexibility. Managers should remind themselves and team members that structure is the servant of the team, not the ruler. All guidelines should be in place to service the team's integrity individually and collectively, but not enslave them with extra work or unnecessary rules.

Sometimes the struggle originates outside the team. Helping the team move through the wall may comprise soliciting additional organizational support for augmenting or creating organizational infrastructures, routines, technological platforms, and tools. A manager's networking and influencing skills are more critical than ever. Jared, for example, saw an opportunity to showcase his team's creative strategies (the ones that resulted from their newfound commitment to one another) by sharing those that had systemic application with the larger organization. The team got to host a web conference for interested organization members on Virtual Work Strategies That Work Around Here. The team got great exposure, the organization had an opportunity to learn together, and the technology enabled the web conference to be captured and posted for later learning for those unable or not ready to attend the conference.

The Virtual Management Competencies

Managing in adaptive, virtual, learning organizations is exhilarating and challenging. The "old" competencies do not become defunct, but expand to a broader leadership and facilitative focus. The remainder of this chapter defines the competencies and commitments that virtual organizations look to their managers to provide for their virtual teams.

Build Commitment, Not Control

Command and control management methods simply do not work in a virtual work environment. There is obviously a place for structure, but not stricture. Build commitment through creating and supporting the shared "sacred" space of the team. Guard the values of the team by modeling and expecting consistency, fairness, and trustworthy action. Rely on everyone in his or her various capacities, regardless of the closest, most convenient person or resource, and expect the same of team members. Expect the spirit of the team to prevail and guide right action. Be scrupulously fair. Begin the team engagement with the trust glass full, and set up consensual agreements that support the glass stay-ing full. Trust is the controller; collaboration is the measure.

As a virtual manager, face the fear of a less controlled environment. Negotiate with yourself and others to find that personal edge—that place where discomfort pushes you to new learning and effectiveness but isn't pushing you over the edge into chaos and panic. Expect com-mitments to be honored and do not settle for excuses. Allow the team to support your management by rotating leadership as appropriate based on experience, desire, competence, or stage of the project. The manager is always the manager, but she can share control through responsibility sharing and agreements.

Focus, Coordinate, and Communicate; Not Authorize, Command, and Plan

The old joke goes, "If you want to hear God laugh, tell him (sic) your plans." An apparently antithetical saying says, "Failure to plan is guar-anteed failure." These are not contradictory; they are both absolutely and paradoxically true. The virtual manager needs to focus and flex, coordinate all the pieces of the game plan without becoming entrenched in how it has to look, and facilitate boundary-crossing com-munication through networks (electronic and people). If a plan is too structured, it will not be able to keep up with the fast-paced market-place demands. If there is no plan, the marketplace will whip the orga-nization and team around much like a garden hose with the water puls-ing out but no manager to "hold the direction."

Workers in the information/knowledge age expect strong leadership and guidance—someone to "hold the direction" of the garden hose. They will not long tolerate, however, rigid commandeering or entitle-ment authority. They want and need focus and structure, but do not perform well with lots of rules and invasive oversight. Virtual teams need a game plan. They want a road map. They look to the virtual manager to keep the eagle eye view on the team mission and how it coordinates with the rest of the organization and with stakeholders. Yet they expect to be included in the formation, management, and adjust-ment of the workflow.

Communicate and facilitate to coordinate resources with technol-ogy and the larger organization and strategic alliances. Provide adequate collaborative tools and team space—virtual and literal. Make sure connectivity links work, and find other needed tools and resources. Your team will value and respect you for it.

Connect, not Gatekeep

A team leader's credibility is directly related to the extensiveness of her network and ability to obtain resources across traditional organizational lines. Networking; keeping people informed; and soliciting input from team members, stakeholders, partners, and customers always will be an integral part of a team leader's job, virtual or not. In a virtual environment it is absolutely critical, especially if the team members are working virtually full time. Virtual managers need to open doors to information and resources and people. They need to ensure that their team members are known by upper management and have the opportunity to work in high profile capacities. They need to make their virtual team "visible" to the organization in whatever ways are necessary in order to guarantee that virtual status does not derail a team member's career path.

This involves networking up, down, and across organizational boundaries, including, at times, outside the traditional organizational walls. The effective virtual manager understands that the idea is to choose actions that make the virtual team and members visible in the organization, regardless of geographic location.

Some fear that with the onset of virtual work and knowledge management infrastructures, the need for middle managers goes away. This couldn't be further from the truth. Middle managers' role as information disseminator changes, but their role as networker, gatekeeper, and conduit between the organization and their teams is more relevant than ever. When a team member's role on a project team is coming to an end, for example, a virtual manager knows this enough in advance to scout for the next "right step" to position, advocate for, and move his team member. Successful career gatekeepers will never want for organizational members willing to serve on teams.

Manage by Results, Not by Sight

It's true that managers can't manage what they can't see . . . using the same techniques in place in many organizations today. The old performance measurement techniques may work, but only if they translate well to a nonvisual and electronically networked environment. Virtual managers must build skills and techniques to manage for results . . . not by sight. New technology and virtual work requires managers to rethink how they've always managed performance. It gives organizations and managers an opportunity to explore and improve the way they have previously managed people and work.

One of the bigger barriers to virtual work has been fear of "How do I know they're really working?" The question that needs to be asked is, "How do I know they're working now?" If you can answer that question, you can usually extrapolate how to know someone is really working in a remote environment. If you don't know how they're working now, then what difference does it make? You have some first steps to take in terms of looking at performance management. The critical part of the question, "How can I manage virtual team performance?" is better reframed, "How do I support collaboration and teamwork so that we reach our targets?"

As Hatim Tyabji, CEO of VeriFone, a 100 percent virtual company, states: "The quid pro quo, in return for all the freedom we offer, is a tremendous emphasis on accountability. We expect you to perform and we expect you to deliver the goods. We don't have any system for lunch breaks. You perform; you can do anything you want. You don't perform; you're out."[25] Team member nonperformance is unacceptable, but so is managerial clock punching. Set realistic performance targets, and manage against the results.

The irony of the original fear-based question, "How do I know they're really working?" is that my experience and research is finding that the *opposite* is true. Virtual employees are working *too* hard, *too* much, and blurring boundaries between home and work. Actually, virtual managers should worry more about helping team members *turn off* work before full burnout occurs. Once burnout sets in, an employee puts in all the hours, but with diminishing returns. Give me a fresh six hours over a stressed and burned-out ten any day!

In fairness to the managers reading this book, distrust is a natural outgrowth of silos, command and control management, and hierar-

---

[25]William C. Taylor, "At Verifone It's a Dog's Life (And They Love It!) (*Fast Company*, November 1995), p. 115.

chies. It is part of the organizational fabric and isn't erased just because the company values state, "We value and trust our employees." If a distrusting culture prevails in the larger organization, trust will not increase or decrease in a virtual environment. Team-specific trust can be built within the team, but it will hit the organizational cultural wall at some point.

Virtual managers can use the systems and feedback loops built by the team during its planning process, allowing the infrastructure itself and the results targeted to be the vehicle for performance monitoring and results management. At the very least, a virtual manager must stop being preoccupied with clock time and start thinking outcomes. Become focused on communication, feedback loops, improving team processes. Let the team and members know the lengths and limits of their authority, deadlines, and how and in what way you as manager need to be involved. Reward collaboration, knowledge sharing, and team learning. Honor those who meet their commitments and responsibilities. Measure results and compensate accordingly.

Coach, Not "Handle"

One of the bigger challenges for the virtual manager is coaching and managing performance without the traditional forms of feedback and face-to-face interaction available on a regular basis. The virtual manager wants to feel comfortable and competent approaching any team member. She also wants to be the person to whom anyone can come for advice, clarification, and assistance with other team members when needed. This holds true for both performance coaching and performance issues as well as developmental coaching.

Observation looks different virtually; it isn't as easy to detect frustration and casually intervene, or see someone putting in long hours and ask what you can do to help. Virtually, the manager seeks the subtle: sharper than usual emails with an almost staccato feel, emails spread throughout the day from 7 A.M. until 10:30 P.M., a curious drop in contacts from two team members. In some ways, the virtual manager becomes almost intuitively sensitive to the subtle. Sometimes it's nothing— the team member is splitting her day in order to spend time with her children after school, hence the early morning and late evening correspondences. Sometimes, however, it signals a warning—a client was unhappy with a milestone deliverable, and the team member doesn't know how to ask for help, thinking he needs to "fix this" by himself.

While observation changes, the basic coaching skills do not change in a virtual environment. An effective coach guides team members into increasingly effective performance without doing it for them. She anticipates problems and conflicts and manages them before they get too big. She is the person to whom a team member usually goes to get back into alignment on a project or for advice and suggestions. This is no different virtually.

Feedback forms do change. Face-to-face is not always an option in virtual organizations. The coaching axiom has always been: give praise publicly and through all media; give constructive feedback privately and in person. The axiom holds true in a virtual environment with the exception of "in person." When possible, face-to-face constructive feedback is still preferred, though it is not always practical. It can be synchronous— "live"—however, and with as much context as possible. Telephone conversations or videoconferences work, unless the team or organizational culture is such that typed feedback is accepted and routine.

One "virtual reality" to keep in mind with asynchronous, one-way feedback is critical. The poorer the context, the fewer "clues" to meaning (facial expression, voice tone, for example), the higher the likelihood of misunderstood meaning. A simple piece of advice via email is more easily misconstrued as harsh than that same advice delivered over lunch and in person. When in doubt, go with the "richest" medium possible and practical.

Dialogue, Not Dictate

Learning organizations require facilitative managers who can help people interact well together with a focus on work and learning/adaptation. Virtual managers create virtual and nonvirtual environments where experience and knowledge is shared through intentional conversation, or dialogue. When people aren't seeing each other every day, active facilitation of opportunities to "discuss" is a vital role for the virtual manager.

The process by which knowledge is made explicit inherently occurs among people. It requires giving people the opportunity and "sacred space" to talk. Talking expands thinking and invites healthy questioning that yields new perspectives. Healthy disagreement and challenge enables teams to question current "truth" in search of a higher and more generative "truth." One of the greatest gifts a manager can offer his virtual team is that of reflection time—dialogue and questioning as legitimate and important work. Encourage team members to explore questions of substance. Invite people into virtual conversations, both synchronous and asynchronous, to ponder and debate and argue together. Attend to everyone's thoughts and opinions, seeking value in every contribution.

This creates true synergy through shared responsibility rather than allowing team members to delegate up the organization, relying on the manager to decide and inform. Get people in the habit of discussing their findings. Let the group determine relevance of data. Encourage wide-ranging networks. Capture learnings as a group, and seek larger implications for other/future projects.

Blend Technology and People, Not Juggle Between

Focus on the people versus focus on the technology is not mutually exclusive. Virtual managers do need to become competent with the technology in order to have a chance at comfortable virtual facilitation, but the focus is still on the people connection. Using the technology to support the people is not only desirable, it is doable. Most of the tools today are user-friendly, so learning to facilitate with collaborative software does not have to demand that managers become technical experts. The real learning for a virtual manager is in understanding the nature of people and teams and the collaborative process.

Remember that in its original meaning "intimacy" did not necessarily mean emotional closeness, but the willingness to pass on honest information. Intimacy can be created and enhanced through multiple vehicles, and the virtual manager needs to become competent in deciding which communication vehicle will best support intimacy in what circumstances. Anonymous polling functions, for example, are great for getting a sense of the group around sensitive issues without asking people to take undue risk. Identified polling lets everyone get a sense for where they are compared to the whole. Chat rooms allow for documented group interaction and slower, more reflective conversation, while audio conferencing allows for freer flow and faster movement.

An audio conference is a terrible vehicle for reflective dialogue; the silence between comments appropriate to dialogue will be confused with silence possibly meaning the member has been unintentionally disconnected from the call. The energy you want to build, the pace you want to move, and the container you want to create are all influenced by the medium. (This is discussed more fully in Chapter 6.)

When goals aren't reached, it is common to assume the context-poor technology is to blame, or to decide that the group settled for less because of the virtual environment. The technology, short of technical failure, is not to blame. Analyzing and adjusting the "relationship" between people and tools is the manager's job. The virtual manager needs to evaluate the design, the facilitation, and the medium choice, but the technology itself is just a tool. It may have been misapplied, or the facilitation may have been clumsy, but the technology itself is neutral. Perhaps people need more training or practice, or they're simply in need of a different environment/medium. Try a videoconference next time, or meet face-to-face, or move the discussion to a listserve. Adjust, don't settle or abandon.

Integrate, Not Comply

Develop and adapt guidelines, workflow processes, and infrastructure to meet the team's needs. Include the larger organization in the picture, especially if it isn't always obvious. Virtual team members can be confused and feel cut off from the organization if there isn't enough connection. They can collectively or individually drift off or become renegades. They may lose their sense of value if the connections aren't clear. A virtual manager needs to help the team feel "embedded" and integrated in the larger organization. Assist team members in integrating their work with the team's work, and the team's work with the organization's work.

Walking the Talk of the Three-Fold Path

When a virtual manager manages from these principles, he is creating and sustaining a cohesive team culture, supporting his team community, and doing his part to ensure that production goals are met. Walking the three-fold path is more an art than a science, and as a learning manager, he gets better with time and practice.

In summary, it is safe to say that there is no one right way to manage a virtual team. Sometimes the manager will need to be very involved in the work or the process functioning of the team, and other times the manager's primary task will be less involved in the team but more involved in the organization—networking, advocating, leading change. The commitment, however, at all times is to purposefully and intentionally support the team and the organization in achieving strategic priorities and fulfilling the charter. Team leadership means always attending to what is happening in the team and the organization and facilitating continuous effectiveness and flow.

The truth is managing a virtual team requires finesse and skill much like facilitating a great meeting or managing a successful project. The successful virtual manager always remembers that facilitating the effective interdependencies of people is key, and all the structures and technologies and systems serve to support the people's involvement, commitment, and satisfaction so they can be effective. When in doubt, ask, *"How can I create, support, and sustain a virtual community so that everyone feels included, involved, and responsible for the collective? How can I tear down silos and walls and create virtual circles?"*

8

LEARNING FROM SOME
TRAILBLAZERS

*You'll find, he remarked gently, "that the only thing you can do
easily is be wrong, and that's hardly worth the effort."*
—*Norman Juster,* The Phantom Tollbooth

Jackson is the team lead for the annual holiday party committee/team.
It is virtual, but members are located close enough to one another that
they meet face-to-face every other month. The holiday party is a huge
celebration each year when awards and honors are presented, and
employees, key customers and vendors, and other stakeholders fly in
from all over to attend. This project team is an additional and volunteer responsibility for all team members, including Jackson, and must
be fit into the rest of their work lives. All, however, are excited about
the party and have expressed a high and ongoing commitment to the
project charter. The team has been working together for ten months.
The organization is strategically committed to virtual work, beginning
with voluntary telecommuting and remote offices. They have barely
embarked on the virtual pathway. Groupware is available to everyone,
but little training has been provided. In some ways, Jackson's team is
pioneering for the organization.

Jackson has led virtual teams in the past, but this is a first time for
the remaining team members. This eight-person team has known one
another for at least 18 months, and several members have worked on

projects together before. All team members are online, but none had participated in online communities or had utilized web conferencing capabilities. The team's comfort level with the technical tools is not high, though all agreed to be open to try new things. All are very comfortable with email and are adjusting very easily to listserves. Only Jackson uses threads as a sorting tool. Jackson tried groupware decision-making support tools a couple times, but people struggled, so he went back to multiple listserve postings.

Jackson has noticed in the last three months that individual team member's habits are taking on "personalities." Paula and Linda are "spurt" communicators. Linda is particularly sporadic. When her responsibilities are coming due, she is very involved, sometimes communicating several times a day. When her part of the project is not the immediate priority, she seems to disappear to the point of not responding even when asked specifically to check in with the team. A couple times Jackson has had to call Linda to reengage her, which has worked each time. Linda then apologizes profusely and gets really involved and "busy" with the team again.

Paula is more routine with her spurts. She checks in a couple times a week, is very active in response to items that may be days old, then checks out again for a few days. This used to irritate Jackson, but he has come to see it as "her way." If he needs an immediate response, he has learned to leave a voicemail asking Paula to check her email.

Vally and Jennifer are very steady virtual team members. They acknowledge all communications, initiate communications when appropriate, and assist the team in keeping with commitments and schedules without being insistent.

Daniel is traditionally aloof. He tends not to volunteer for task forces or other volunteer commitments, although he is a highly competent and committed organizational member. His professional responsibilities require very little time on the computer, and virtually no time online. When he volunteered for this committee, Jackson and the team were surprised and delighted. Daniel has become completely inactive in the listserve and only shows up to meetings occasionally.

Brian was holiday party chair last year and is continuing this year in an advisory capacity. He occasionally responds to a group message or provides support or clarification, but for the most part, he has made it clear that he is not an active committee member. All have agreed that is appropriate to his role, and no one suggests that he take on any responsibilities. His contributions are welcome when they are offered.

Petra has been on the party committee in the past, although it was not a virtual team previously. She is the "history" of the committee as well as a committed current team member. At the same time, Jackson knows that Petra is the first to volunteer for anything and tends to overextend herself. This would not be a problem because she always shows up for every meeting, except that she isn't always quick to respond to a request. In the last two months, Jackson has noticed that this has gotten even worse. Several team members are asking repeatedly for information from Petra, and no one is hearing from her. Jackson doesn't know if there's a personal problem interfering, nor does he feel comfortable pushing her too hard since this is a volunteer project. At the same time, other team members are getting very frustrated because she is missing in action, and that is preventing critical milestones from being met.

At the last face-to-face meeting, Jackson addressed these concerns with the group, and he suggested they collectively revisit the communication infrastructure and protocol agreements they had made. Several team members had let protocols slip, and Jackson suggested the group recommit or adjust to the commitments. The outcomes were many heartfelt apologies, a collective recommitment to the group and to the protocols, and everyone parting ways feeling better about each other and the team.

Now Jackson is seeing the same symptoms reappearing. In fact, he's not sure they ever stopped. Yet the project is getting done, the team really enjoys getting together, especially face-to-face, and everyone is having fun. What does he do?

Bad habits and practices in traditional work settings often get exacerbated in virtual work environments, and new risks are introduced. From organizational and team perspectives, this chapter identifies warning signs that problems are likely to occur, how to prevent them from occurring, how to recognize them when they do, and what to do about them to get back on track quickly.

Program Implementation Components—
Lessons Learned

Telecommuting Success, Inc. and TSI Services,[26] two companies dedicated to successful implementation of virtual work solutions, asked several dozen organizational leaders and virtual work program managers to identify what program implementation components helped or hurt their success. Most initiatives were begun internally without external assistance, and the driving functions were usually information technology or human resources. In a few cases, facilities (real estate shortage) drove the change, but the implementation was delegated to the human resources function. Companies being interviewed had a virtual work process in place for at least one year. We asked them to focus on lessons learned from a systemwide perspective. Several common themes recurred in almost every case to one degree or another.

1. Overwhelmingly, most stated that their organizations had failed to give adequate consideration to the *cultural impact* of distributed work and teams. By not addressing the critical component of culture, they slowed significantly their company's ability to quickly adapt to a virtual environment. Perquisites ("perks") were a particularly prominent example of cultural barriers. For example, one very large global organization faced resistance to telecommuting specifically because in their culture the size of the employee's office and the floor on which it was located was an indication of stature in the organization. If an employee moved his office to his home, how would anyone know how important he was? Work has to be done to change perceived status in the organization before career-minded individuals will embrace a virtual work solution.

2. Organizations found limited success when they took a temporary or fragmented approach to virtual work. When companies embarked on "pilot programs" to *"see if telecommuting and other remote work team options worked,"* programs succeeded,

---

[26]This author and several colleagues conducted this research over approximately a three-year period, from 1996 to 1998.

but only in pockets or very slowly. Looking back, most agreed that they should not have "piloted" virtual work because it sent a message to the organization members:

- This may turn out to be another management fad.
- We don't know if it works ourselves.
- You're taking a risk with your career if you get attached to a failure.

This not only wasn't the message they wanted to send, it also skewed program success. If participants in the pilot programs had requested or volunteered to become virtual employees, the pilots were hugely successful. The pilot participants were people who really wanted to work virtually, and they were willing to do almost anything to make it succeed. When the program was then expanded and less enthusiastic employees were put in virtual situations, the real support barriers and struggles became obvious because the employees were less inclined to make it work regardless, especially if career visibility suffered because organizational supports and systems were not in place to support virtual worker career paths.

What they should have done instead, and, on hindsight, many stated they would have done instead, is clearly say that they were not piloting virtual work per se, but piloting *how to make it work in this organization*. This sends a very different message about committing to virtual work, while acknowledging a period of time to debug the process for *this organization*.

3. Inadequate resources, support, and training were provided to the virtual workers. Those organizations that provided training in the virtual environment, remote management, and in using the technology had far greater, faster success than those that did not. Additionally, the organizations that provided specific assistance—technical help desk, coaching or other ongoing support, and assistance in setting up a virtual office, for example—found their virtual employees rated their job satisfaction much higher than those who did feel they received adequate support. It is important that virtual employees and managers take some responsibility for

success, but the primary responsibility remains with the company. Nothing interferes more with one's ability to be highly productive than having to figure out a whole new "job" called virtual work. Provide training and support up front, and productivity and job satisfaction have a much greater chance of remaining high.

4. Expansion of virtual work beyond pockets or pilots was hampered by not having a plan for sustainability. For example, a company in New England had a few dozen virtual workers operating in a telecommuting environment. All lived relatively close to the traditional office. When any virtual employee had computer breakdowns or technical difficulties, one technical support employee who happened to love riding his motorcycle would ride to the telecommuter's home and do an on-site repair. This worked well for everyone concerned—until it was time to expand the virtual work initiative beyond a few dozen people. The organization had no plan in place for program expansion. The technical support person got very quickly overwhelmed, and he couldn't sustain the level of effective support that had worked so well for the few.

5. Companies also acknowledged unnecessary reinvention of the wheel. Virtual teams "discovered" their own ways, means, habits, and templates for effective communication, connection, and production. Some teams obviously did a better job of this than others. What was NOT in place were vehicles to mine effective strategies from the micro level (team specific) and avail them to the macro organizational level so that teams could learn from one another instead of having to figure everything team by team by team.

    This hits upon the need for networked organizations to become and remain learning organizations. In co-located environments, at least in most organizations I have been in, people learn by happenstance, informal mentoring, and by being in the right place at the right time. One asks the question of the person closest by who can help, or learning is available through invitation to a meeting or task force because it's part of one manager's idea of a career opportunity. In other words, if we're honest, a lot of learning is accidental. In virtual teams, employees are dispersed globally or in different branches, or in their homes. That accidental learning doesn't take place, so there needs to be an intentional knowledge sharing process. It needs to be more intentional. Companies need to address this dilemma early on, if they're growing, want to remain vibrant, and "grow" their organizational members in a virtual environment.

6. The last program implementation component that companies identified as hurting their success was a poor kick-off and communication plan and inadequate attention to change management. Virtual work changes not only the way the organization works, but also the way the individuals and teams work. People want to know what it means; why it matters; how it impacts their day, their life, and their career. Organizations that prepared people well, educated them about the opportunities, and acted with integrity (aligned actions with statements) had early success that was more easily expanded to a sustainable initiative. A previous chapter outlines one company's commitment to an effective kick-off and communication campaign.

    Change management went beyond a two-hour training module on change. It included an honest willingness to assess systems and infrastructures to better align the organization as a system with a virtual teaming environment. In other words, the successful organizations put their systems where their mouths were. The *organization* was willing to change.

The Impact of Virtuality on Feedback Loops

Cause and effect are not usually closely related in time and space, even in a traditional work environment, yet we problem solve as though they were. If there is a problem with sales, we provide incentives for sales people to "try harder." If customers are on hold too long with the customer service call center, we reward telephone service representatives for handling customers faster. In a complex system, however, the cause for the effect isn't usually that linear. Sales may be down because word has gotten out to the user community that follow-up telephone support is slow, and what support is provided is rushed. (Okay, so that was too simple, but it makes the point.) By assuming a cause and effect that is linear or closely linked (e.g., sales are down because of the sales staff), the organization doesn't look for the larger feedback loops that link true causes with true effects.

Add time and geographical distance, and the "distance" between cause and effect may become even greater, and the feedback loop is delayed even more. Delays can cause organizations to badly overshoot their mark. Distant cause-and-effect relationships that go unrecognized could cause organizations to shoot at the wrong target altogether. Knowing this is armor and provides the organization with high leverage for preventing system breakdowns. Eliminate systems delays as much as possible, or, if they cannot be eliminated, recognize them and adjust by being more patient with the feedback loops. Consciously link causes and geographically distance effects, or at least be conscious of the impact distance may have on relationships. The same holds true for "time distance" effects.

At the team level, the distance of time and distance is also a concern. In a virtual team, when things go awry, they can do so for a longer period of time before they're noticed, so the virtual team leader—or any team member, but particularly the team leader—must be more vigilant to catch early warning signs of a problem with the team or the schedule. A missed target can go undetected longer because of the time-geography delays that are natural to a virtual team. The problem is not usually intention or commitment to the team. It's usually some breakdown of communication or feedback loop. This is true in any group of people coming together, and it's exacerbated in a virtual environment.

Eliminating or reducing delays doesn't have to be a Big Brother control device, however. It is best remedied by practicing the tenets of this book and building relationships and communication infrastructures that intentionally create and sustain commitment and connection. Just know that when you've got people co-located, red flags are more obvious. Virtually, unless attention is paid, problems can go on a day or two or a week longer than they would otherwise.

At the Team Level, How Will I Know When It's Not Working?

When problems erupt in a virtual team, the problem is not usually willingness, inability to use the technology, cultural differences, inability to handle conflict, or virtual work itself. Rather, the problem is usually erosion of mutual trust, hidden conflict that has gone unaddressed or unrecognized, poor information and communication management, or nonaligned systems and structures. Let's examine the warning signs of virtual teaming issues, as well as possible causes for the symptomatic warning signs.

Symptomatic Warning Signs

Direction and focus are confusing. Miscommunication, lack of feedback, and making different assumptions about what matters are signs that the team charter is no longer clear and the virtual environment has allowed the lack of alignment to go undetected or without response, increasing the virtual distance between members. Project pieces are not coordinating smoothly. The team is experiencing or creating frequent direction switches, often without warning or reasoning. Frequent arguments erupt about what the team should do next. These symptoms indicate that the workflow process or communication infrastructure has fallen apart, is not being utilized, or was not clearly defined in the first place.

Team members in deciding how to move forward or if they should speak up exercise *excessive caution*. Normally outspoken team members are withdrawn. Work products are timidly introduced. Unfortunately, people can be crueler in a faceless environment. Sometimes people forget that words still have impact, whether they are said in person or in text, and email bullying results. "Plops" occur out of the blue, harsh words are not tempered with the context of a soft voice or a smile, rushed statements are tossed into cyberspace without much thought to how they might be received. Attention to the interpersonal impact of language and tone cannot be stressed enough in a virtual environment.

Information problems show up in a variety of ways.

- Team members are not sharing quickly or fully. Information is being hoarded or not being intentionally shared often because the by-the-way water cooler habit has not been recreated in a virtual environment, or because the organization rewards hoarding. If information is shared reluctantly or partially, team effectiveness suffers even more in a virtual environment since "accidental" discovery is less likely to occur. This creates workflow slowdowns or bottlenecks, frustration on the part of other team members, and, eventually, trust issues as discussed elsewhere in this book. Not sharing quickly or fully interferes with team and organizational learning as well, and severely limits the effectiveness of the knowledge sharing process.

- The reverse, information obesity, can be another clue to virtual team problems. The database doesn't hold all the latest information, or holds so many versions of the same information that it is difficult to use. Too much email, too much saved information, too many versions of a document, long list serve threads that have not been "pruned," too many people being copied into correspondence—all indicate a lack of prioritization, inadequate information processing protocols, or excessive caution. Information obesity coming primarily from one person also indicates that a team member may be feeling isolated and looking for some forced acknowledgment, recognition, or reassurance.

Conflict goes underground. Sometimes people are being *too* nice, and there isn't enough healthy difference of opinion. Most people are not comfortable with conflict, and the virtual environment sometimes makes it easier to let conflict go underground and remain hidden. It then seems to erupt suddenly, but it usually has been boiling. Low-touch communication leads to miscommunication and misunderstood messages. There is a significantly increased risk of misconstrued messages because of the media, and unintentionally trust can be broken as a result. If trust is low, conflict is more likely to be explosively unproductive or go underground. "Failure to perform" can be the result of withdrawal from participation rather than commitment to engage in healthy conflict management. Part of the team development task needs to be to create ground rules for surfacing process issues.

What Is Jackson to Do?

Jackson is committed to collaborative teamwork, and in many ways supports the party planning virtual team in being a self-managing team. He believes in making it easy for people to do the right thing. What he has noticed is that some team members are making commitments to the team based on where they *wish* to be, rather than where they are currently performing. The team is meeting its commitments. They're just not doing so as efficiently as they could because of the inconsistent follow-through on commitment to the communication protocols and the resulting need to communicate with people in other ways—redundantly. Jackson sees these as workarounds that are accommodating poor habits, yet he is doing it himself in order to meet commitments and deadlines.

Jackson realized that for several team members, the reluctance to follow protocol (such as utilizing decision-making support software) was more of a comfort issue than willingness. He invited the team to participate in an online community web party. He offered to write a very brief training aid to walk people through the steps of participation; he would "attend" the party with them, and they could "lurk" without participating. This enabled them to experience the tools without the expectation of having to participate unless they wanted to. Four team members participated, and, as a result, they were much less intimidated by the tools. Of course, ideally the organization would have provided groupware and other tool training, but, as stated previously, virtual work is in its infancy for this company. Jackson took it upon himself to assist his teammates. Down the road, in keeping with the precepts of a learning organization, a similar experiential exposure is in the organization's training plan. Jackson has volunteered to be a virtual work mentor/guide.

Jackson also took some time to analyze his team's communication patterns. Because of personal comfort and organizational culture, his team was most comfortable when communication was face-to-face. Email quickly became the most common communication vehicle, followed by face-to-face. Telephone calling was used seldom, although more so with Petra because that's how she was reachable, and with Paula occasionally when she needed to be reengaged with the team. The email, face-to-face, and phone were adequate to get the job done. He relaxed and accepted that comfort came with practice, and willingness came with no pressure to perform. He began to enjoy leading this team again, while still nudging increasing virtuality.

Jackson realized that it was the connection created with face-to-face meetings that made the online communication in between meetings sufficient. The group really looked forward to meeting in person, and often carried on continuing social conversation online for days after meetings. People used to "save" pictures and other fun sharings for when they got together. Over the months, however, Jackson sent a few pictures to the group as .jpg files, and this prompted a higher level of ongoing social commitment among the group. Others began asking for pictures. The work was still getting done, and people were having fun. The connection was no longer "saved" for in-person get-togethers; it was ongoing.

If face-to-face communication had not been an option and web conferencing were used exclusively, the team would either step to the plate or fail. Jackson and the organization would have to provide training, and the team management would have to be more strictly tied to the protocols. Jackson's team made choices based on culture and success. If Jackson's team had not been succeeding, he might have needed to do more than nudge.

What about the other team issues, however? Daniel had been MIA for awhile. After several requests from several members, Paula realized that Daniel simply did not respond online. She called Daniel and clarified his willingness and ability to "rejoin" the group. Daniel agreed to attend the party, but that his personal preference to not join committees, the difficulty in finding time to log in, and his travel schedule precluded his participation. And he disliked email. He had accepted it as reality, but elected not to participate in virtual teams when he had a choice. The group thanked him for his honesty and released him from all team responsibilities.

The team caringly confronted Paula and Linda on their "spurts," and the group renegotiated frequency of check-in. At first they simply agreed to meet the protocol, but Jackson kindly pointed out that a doable commitment that was less than originally hoped for by the team was infinitely preferable to the team than another round of commitments that would not be met. Paula and Linda met the group halfway, and it has been working.

Jackson has relaxed his desire to become fully virtual, and, in fact, recognizes that he loves the face-to-face interaction as well. He identified a team fear that if they did all their work virtually, that they would have no need to meet face-to-face. He helped the group see that becoming increasingly effective virtually would not replace face-to-face meetings, but would decrease how much face time would need to be spent on logistics and "admistrivia." This hidden barrier to virtual effectiveness, once unearthed and addressed, eliminated almost all conscious and unconscious resistance.

Petra is still not honoring her online communication commitments, but the group has shifted her responsibilities so fewer bottlenecks can result. Her strengths on-site at the party, as well as her enthusiasm and creativity are too valuable to lose. The team decided to capitalize on her strengths that give her and others the most joy, and agreed to call her on her cell phone. She was still on the listserve, but no one expected her to respond unless she was "told" by phone to go online and respond.

Did the group accommodate her? Yes, but it was consensually agreed to because the team values her contribution so much that the compromise is worth it. The team created a wonderful holiday event and is fully committed to continuing on the project team for next year. Jackson couldn't be happier. True story.

Other Virtual Tips to Avoid Traps

- Accept some loss of operational efficiency. This doesn't always happen, but it's less frustrating when a certain "acceptable slippage" is allowed. It will be regained in other areas, like speed of message delivery.

- For some team members, who are used to being on teams and are good team players, to move to a virtual team can be a bit jolting at first. One reason this jolt occurs is that if it's a true team with a lot of interaction, a synergy results. Synergy does happen with virtual teams as well, but there isn't always that extroverted high. Build that intentionally through some other ways discussed elsewhere in this book.

- One problem with asynchronous communication is dissipation of group energy. The team can start to drift apart without regular contact. Creative brainstorming can fall flat if not moved along. Team leaders must help the group feel that it is together. Other chapters explore this more fully, but one example here is organize the group around brainstorming ideas or questions to pursue, and divide into virtual spaces for breakout groups similar to those that occur in face-to-face sessions.

- Focusing too much on rules and procedures provides an illusion of certainty, but in the absence of any mechanism to enforce or monitor, it really just creates a Big Brother feeling. Structure is a servant, not a master. Treat it as such.

- Acknowledge the occupational and cultural differences among the team members, while developing *"this team's culture."*

- Team leaders must be *scrupulously fair.* Avoid temptation to rely on the closest person or resource. Have the *entire team in mind,* not just the team members seen regularly. Attend to all team members' needs, opinions, and contributions.

- Confront all nonperformance. Management responsibilities do not lessen in a virtual environment.

- Make a special effort to catch conflicts early and deal with them fairly. If there are miscommunications and they don't get acknowledged and remedied, it can lead to trust issues. Again, this can happen whether a team is virtual or it's not, but in a virtual environment, trust issues sometimes go unrecognized, unaddressed, and unresolved far too long, because **they can.** In a virtual environment, it's easier just to sweep conflict under the rug until it becomes a much bigger issue and can't be ignored anymore. *Don't be tempted.*

  The bad news for team leaders is that commitment to the team and the team mission decreases if conflict goes unresolved. The good news is that resolved and well-managed conflict can clear the way for increased team commitment. If unhealthy conflict goes undetected or unresolved for too long, team members *will* look around for alternatives.

- Since high productivity and effectiveness is the bottom line for any organization, it is the virtual manager's responsibility to do whatever it takes to create a work environment for productivity and effectiveness to happen.

Most, if not all, of the early warning signs of virtual problems can be prevented or managed by coming back to the team's development process which clarifies purpose, commitment, and systems. The second key prevention and resolution strategy is, again, to commit to the three-fold path of creating a cohesive team culture, supporting the team community, and producing successful outcomes.

SECTION FOUR

ORGANIZATIONALLY DISPERSED

CONNECTIONS TO THE FUTURE

In times of change, the learners inherit the earth while the learned find themselves beautifully equipped to live in a world that no longer exists.

—Eric Hoffer

Don't be afraid to take a big step if one is indicated. You can't cross a chasm in two small jumps.

—David Lloyd George

9

THE EVOLVING
PARTNERSHIP OF VIRTUAL
TEAMING WITH
KNOWLEDGE MANAGEMENT

I use not only all the brains I have, but all I can borrow.
—Woodrow Wilson

The organizations that will truly excel in the future will be the organizations that discover how to tap people's commitment and capacity to learn at ALL levels in an organization.
—*Peter Senge,* The Fifth Discipline

Virtual Teams as Building Blocks
for Organizational Learning

Organizational transformation can only occur if change becomes part of a new way of "doing things around here"—the culture. And embedding change involves organizational learning. This is truer in the knowledge age than ever before. In fact, intellectual capital is as or more important to business today as any other form of capital—real estate, equipment, and inventory, for example. Today, to not manage organizational knowledge is as irresponsible as not managing the budget or inventory. Organizations must leverage learning across all areas of the business and strategic relationships. The successful organization is built on its ability to use and manage knowledge. In other words, organizations are built on their ability to *learn.*

Knowledge, however, is a capital asset *only* if the organization *can* learn. Information only becomes true organizational knowledge when it is processed and embedded in routines, systems, processes, and organizational culture, which enables progressive action.[27] Knowledge management goes beyond the capture, storage, and retrieval of information. It is a way of helping the organization unbury the hidden treasures of knowledge that lie in people's minds (tacit knowledge), and make that knowledge accessible to a larger group of individuals who are responsible for acting and deciding in the best interest of the organization. The virtual environment provides an incredible opportunity to capture knowledge through informal exchange among team members because much of the exchange is captured through email, web conferencing, bulletin boards, and chat rooms and other discussion forums. Effective managers of virtual teams can catalyze learning for their group by asking questions, challenging members to question perspectives, and continuing to push the dialogue. They can then catalyze learning for the organization by connecting the team's learning to the greater whole through various means. Once again, the whole becomes greater than the sum of its parts.

As more organizations are at least partially virtual, the virtual manager's ability to manage the relationship between knowledge management and virtual team collaboration becomes even more critical. As organizations identify and develop emerging leaders who are geographically dispersed, mentoring and leadership development need to become increasingly virtual as well. This chapter explores these issues and provides practical guidelines and minimum requirements of a knowledge sharing program as it applies in a virtual environment.

Winning Hearts and Minds in the Spirit of Generosity and Responsibility: A Metaphor

Generosity is not a particularly common word in business today, and yet, isn't a spirit of generosity an essential part of sharing intellectual

---

[27]Paul S. Meyer, ed., *Knowledge Management and Organization Design* (Boston: Butterwork-Heinemann Press, 1997).

capital? Historically, organizational employees developed their valu
their organizations in no small part based on what they knew, and th.ʼ
futures were secured by becoming indispensable because of that knowledge. Magic wand waving will not change that historical truth at all,
let alone overnight. Building organizational systems that support and
reinforce knowledge sharing, however, *can* change perceptions, motivations, and behavior. These are the same organizational systems that
support and reinforce virtual teaming. The synergies are natural.

Think of the organization as a living system, as a human body. The
body is the living system of the organization, the parts coming together
into a living whole. People can become increasingly competent at thinking and working together in ways that support organizational learning.
What makes that system work, however, as it applies to breathing the
spirit of generosity and responsibility into the virtual body?

The Bones

No body can hold together without a basic skeleton to provide a frame.
The bones that drive an organization are the systems and infrastructure, and more particularly how they drive *incentives* and *rewards*, that
which reinforces behavior. People do what they get reinforced for
doing. If you want to support generous sharing of knowledge across
functional boundaries, then reward it. Do not acknowledge excellence
based on unique expertise; rather, expand excellence by rewarding the
sharing and spreading of that expertise.

The Heart

The body has major organs, all contributing to the overall functioning of the body. While all are important and even sometimes redundant (we have two lungs and kidneys, for example, while we only
need one lung or kidney), one cannot live long without a heart. The
heart of an organization is the *commitment of the people*. Leaders
and managers must continually create meaning in the workplace.
Without it, little innovation, learning, and sharing will occur naturally. Help people create a committed vision of a collaborative,
knowledge sharing and virtual culture, then "backbone" it with
aligned incentives and rewards, and the heart will pump life force
throughout the system.

The Muscle

Now it's time to put the "meat on the bones." The muscle of *responsibility* and *accountability* gives the body strength to do what it says it wants to do. Organizational, management, team, and individual responsibility builds strength for the system.

The Arteries

The *technology* of interactive databases and groupware are the arteries of the virtual organizational body. The networked blood vessels are interlinked to carry the organizational life force to every part of the system's living body. Knowledge is shared, captured, catalogued, and communicated throughout the virtual system. The focus is on using people and information technology to further embed a culture of knowledge sharing built on relationships and trust.

The Lifeblood

Until blood flows through the body, it is not alive. *Dialogues* and *communication* are the lifeblood of the organizational body. People talking to people, through various means, are still an essential ingredient for a living, breathing being. Free flowing communication, like unblocked blood flow, builds a healthy, oxygenated organizational body.

Building Shared Meaning

Transforming individual or team knowledge into organizational knowledge requires designing bones, muscles, and arteries where people find it easy, comfortable, and rewarding to share what they know. It is important that this not be an extra burden of work responsibility, but an extension of a natural conversation and updates occurring between or among people. People need to *want* to give forth, rather than hold back.

Virtual work provides an opportunity (or a challenge) to the building of shared meaning. Traditionally, especially in mentor relationships, knowledge is transferred primarily in person to whoever is close by and connected to the knowledge holder. Without intentionally reaching out, and without the support of technology, the knowledge transfer across geography suffers. Just as books aren't learned by osmosis by putting them under our pillows at night, tacit knowledge isn't transferred by osmosis in a virtual environment. (It isn't really transferred by osmosis in a co-located environment, but informal and natural conversation may be so invisible as a "learning forum" that it appears so.)

It would be unfair to say that virtual work does not place a greater demand on knowledge management. Deliberate networks and infrastructures must be created if they are not in place already. The communication infrastructure created for the virtual team should be aligned with the knowledge management/sharing infrastructure of the larger organization. This doesn't, however, need to be a huge enterprise, or done all at once.

Begin by looking at how knowledge sharing is currently done in your organization, what tools and infrastructure are already in place, however informal, and see how they function or need to be expanded or replaced in an electronically networked virtual world. In other words, enable what still works in a virtual work world, enhance what can continue to work with modifications, and create what does not yet exist. Virtual teams tend to develop new tools as needed, voluntarily and informally, anyway. As these tools get honed, they usually have generalized application and can be shared with the larger organization, and may become widespread. This, in essence, is knowledge sharing at its finest in a learning organization.

A collaborative knowledge sharing culture encourages interactions at many organizational levels and across teams. People choose with whom they need to communicate without the limitation of boundary, title, distance, or time. In other words, organizational members are responsible for creating their own learning networks to exchange information, find expertise, and pool resources and talent. These intricate and personal networks (especially when supported by knowledge capturing technology and collaborative software) facilitate knowledge transfer within and among virtual teams. Organizations and virtual managers can help this along by creating mechanisms for outreach and communication.

Learning Is Individual and Collective

Training and development functions are often thought of as the "learning center" of an organization. Learning does occur through training, development, and mentoring. The focus in this model, however, is on the individual as the learner rather than the larger collective, whether it is a team or the entire organization. Thinking this way limits learning to an individual responsibility. While learning *is* an individual responsibility, it is also a "group" responsibility to learn and support learning. A more important question to ask is, "What does the group need to learn in order to fulfill its charter?" Now there is shared responsibility among the many for supporting everyone's learning needs. Learning is focused on practical mission accomplishment.

As common is the belief that information technology is the "information center" of the organization. Working in a culture of knowledge sharing—of giving forth rather than holding back—is not possible without a strong IT function that enables communication technologies that support interaction. At the same time, a healthy virtual "body" doesn't happen just because the arteries are clear. The people sharing and using the information are the ones who convert information to knowledge, and from which good decisions and work gets done. Every member of the collective organizational body is the true information center. IT provides the tools to disseminate and move it, as well as provides the "container" for archival databases.

Innovation is a critical success factor in most organizations, and innovation is more likely to occur in a learning organization. Rosabeth Moss Kanter,[28] when discussing the organizational requirements to foster innovation, states that innovation is more likely when organizational structures and culture value diversity, multiple networks both inside and outside the organization, belief in and unleashing of people's talents, collaboration and teamwork. In order to actualize these values requires organizational structures to be more flexible so that individuals and teams can network and interlink in multiple ways.

We've already discussed how organizations that are structurally aligned around function or specialty, as many organizations are today, are at a disadvantage in a virtual environment. Moss Kanter states that creativity is also stifled. What builds successful virtual organizations

---

[28]Paul S. Meyer, ed., *Knowledge Management and Organization Design* (Boston: Butterwork-Heinemann Press, 1997).

also produces innovation. The more people can build and sustain rela-tionships, the more sources of information and insight they can access.

For the astute reader, strangely familiar themes are being heard—criteria for a functioning team correlate to criteria for a successful vir-tual organization, which correlate to a vital knowledge management process, which supports a learning organization. What works? Net-worked organizations, shared responsibility, dialogue and open com-munication, boundary crossing, wide access, teams.

The Magic Word Is . . . "Network"

So we need to network. What does that mean? Of course, there's the technical component of networking. What, though, does developing "intricate and personal networks" really mean in a virtual knowledge management context? In *Knowledge in Organizations,*[29] Krackhardt discusses three types of relationship networks, each obvious by its name: advice, trust, and communication.

Advice and trust networks look not only at the mentoring channels in the organization, but political alliances and struggles as well. Who talks to whom about what kinds of work? Who trusts whom with what kind of information or advice? Mapping networks can uncover those "knowledge rich" and trusted individuals that many turn to for wisdom, and from whom the organization will want to "pull" knowledge in order to embed the wisdom in organizational knowledge. Mapping advice networks can also unveil where political realities in an organization will support or not support recommended changes (such as movement to an increasingly vir-tual environment). Analyzing communication networks can help identify information flow gaps, redundant resources, and bottlenecks.

Knowledge Management for Dummies[30]

Organizations today do not lack information. They may lack the tools to get the right information to the right people at the right time

---

[29]Laurence Prusak, ed., *Knowledge in Organizations* (Boston: Butterwork-Heinneman, 1997).
[30]The source book I used to provide definitions and write a *very* brief overview of knowledge management is *Knowledge Management Tools,* edited by Rudy L. Ruggles, III (Boston: Butterwork-Heinemann Press, 1997).

and in a way that it can become knowledge. The field of knowledge management is dedicated to improving the movement of information and creation of organizational knowledge. "Knowledge" includes process knowledge (how to do something), catalog knowledge (how to identify what is), and experiential knowledge (knowing based on what has happened). Knowledge management covers three main knowledge activities: generation, codification, and transfer. All three types of knowledge (process, catalog, and experiential) are similarly generated, codified, and transferred.

Let's further define the three knowledge activities.

1. Knowledge generation includes all activities which bring to light knowledge which is "new," whether it is new to one person, a team, an organization, or the world through true discovery.

2. Knowledge codification is the capture and representation of knowledge so that it can be moved from one location/person to another in a way that it can be absorbed.

3. Transfer is the methodology for movement of the knowledge.

Transfer of knowledge in an organization typically falls broadly into four common methodologies:

1. Learning (all forms of training and self-study)

2. Advice (internal consultants, mentors, expert systems, online and help desks, online bulletin boards)

3. Information (online references, manuals and job aids, and other intranet and Internet access points)

4. Tools (applications such as performance support and collaborative groupware)

The real purpose of knowledge management is not to build knowledge *tools* but to build *knowledge*. The real purpose of virtual work is not to *allow distance* but to *create synergy* for mission accomplishment *without the limitations* of time or space. Virtual teams should access and use all transfer methodologies available to them, and they can build their communication infrastructures around their organization's mechanisms and methodologies.

It is important to note that "knowledge" is not a collection of static factoids. It is alive—always changing, growing, evolving—and must be constantly attended. Advanced knowledge tools allow some context to be captured along with content, making information richer and more obviously relevant. The better the tools, the easier it is for virtual teams to use them to create global workspaces. Conversely, the more virtual teams collaborate, the more rich information gets fed back into building the organization's knowledge through using the tools. Both the human commitment and tool robustness are necessary. They work and evolve together.

This is not to say knowledge management is a science, or that every nugget of knowledge will, can, or should be fully captured. We're dealing with human beings, and human beings are organic systems that can never be fully "defined." The memory of organizations, too, is inconsistent. Knowledge becomes nested within other knowledge, but not all events are recorded or even remembered. Sometimes knowledge that is stored is not always easy to retrieve. Just like an Internet search engine, intranet interactive search findings for specific knowledge are based on how frequently the site was accessed, or how recently. The rules and structures of the tools are getting more flexible, but they are still unbendable attempts to anticipate and capture human thought process, which is inherently very bendable and not altogether amenable to following clear linear rules.

So if the tools are limited, why do this? Moving data to geographically dispersed teams is the only thing that makes sense in a virtual world. People feel more informed and are more in charge of how and when they access the information. They feel less out of the organizational information loop. The broader access to information and to people (who hold knowledge) expands people's potential. In other words, I cannot talk in person regularly to as many people as I can with email conversation. I cannot go to a library and find, sort, and analyze as much information in the same amount of time as I can by conducting an Internet search.

Another benefit is that responsibility for learning and knowing can be shared and placed at the most relevant level(s). Stakeholders can be informed without having to participate in a training or meeting. Learners can learn when and as they need rather than having to wait for a seminar or other time-bound event. It provides a collaborative environment for work and learning, which obviously is harmonious with global, virtual work and organizational community building.

Managing organizational knowledge is a responsibility of every organizational member. All are leaders and managers of learning. All are responsible for collaboration, virtual work, and continuous learning. Two of the guiding virtual management principles from Chapter 7 have applications for knowledge management as well. Organizational leadership can support collaborative learning by focusing on the following areas.

Building Commitment, Not Control

The entire knowledge management process is a delicate balance between "rules" and flexibility. It works better when it is facilitated rather than controlled; yet controls can help automate simple decisions and guide people in decision making. With knowledge management, embedding knowledge into the controls, which works if the information is reliable and robust, does this. This is easier when the information being posted and pulled out is quantifiable, undeniable, and not open to personal bias. For example, a city government has committed to a coaching model that they want every supervisor to use. A training aid was developed delineating the seven-step process of performance problem analysis, followed by the five-step coaching intervention guidelines. This training aid can be accessed any time by, for example, a new supervisor when deciding how to move forward with an employee who misses every deadline.

On the other hand, excessive rules for how to input and retrieve information can quickly undo a great idea. For example, if contributing to the knowledge base is tedious and extra work, people will shy away from doing it, if only from a sheer time shortage. If too many or too few controls are in place to pull information, a search may yield nothing useful or too much information, resulting in frustration or overload.

Some standard operating procedures need to be very carefully and thoughtfully put in place so that pushing or pulling information is easy and useful. There are, however, many less quantifiable aspects of knowledge management. Who will decide what information meets accuracy standards? What if information is posted as fact when, in fact, it is opinion? In fact, who decides what is fact and what is opinion? As new discovery is made, how does "more accurate" knowledge replace outdated knowledge? All these questions are not the focus of this book, but they do pose the practical and philosophical questions.

One has to question the quality and validity of what they find on the Internet. Much great information is out there, and much misinformation. Discernment is the key. In an internal knowledge management process, technical rules and controls will never replace our need to think for ourselves. Organizations sometimes want to control for every risk, every variable, every possible information mutation. It is understandable and tempting to gravitate toward imposing a command and control structure on new technology despite the inappropriate fit. Risk of poor information does need to be managed, but the risk of forcing inappropriate rules on individual and organization "thought" is probably a greater one. Organizations would better serve themselves and their people by focusing on helping people exercise good judgment.

Connecting, Not Gatekeeping

Effective knowledge management processes promote a natural and informal information flow that is fast, and pushes and pulls information. The human and technical elements promote creation of common cognitive ground through providing context, thereby increasing its richness. For example, a virtual team is formed for a fast-start crisis-driven project operating with a very tight deadline. They create a communication infrastructure that is real time, efficient, and effective. They post this process for other teams to be able to access. What they realize is that their particular infrastructure was effective in their context based on purpose, need, and speed. It would not be the best choice for a different kind of virtual team such as, for example, a committee exploring the need to set policies for corporate Internet usage. In posting the infrastructure, the posting also includes background on the team, the team purpose, and suggestions for appropriate application. They might also identify one or two contacts for those seeking further information.

Knowledge management isn't just about people's use of the technology. It's also about relationships and building human networks.

More contact with people increases the likelihood that knowledge sharing will occur. Temporary team member swaps on temporary duty is one option that broadens experience and builds relationships across boundaries. With several clients, when a virtual team has been less effective, the individuals on the team have leaned too far in one of three directions. They have been overly reliant on each other, thereby not linking enough to other teams or the rest of the organization, and forming a semi-closed system; or they have been overly reliant individually on other individuals outside their team, thereby never really committing to their own team. The third scenario is when the individual team members are overly dependent on one team member, usually the manager, to be the connector among them.

Managers help virtual teams and knowledge sharing succeed by encouraging cross pollination, expansive networks, while still nurturing the team's interdependence.

In summary, by setting out to manage knowledge, to represent what people know and make it accessible, organizations turn individual knowledge into an organizational asset. The walls of geographical closeness as a criterion for mentoring fall. Virtual team members lose the need to fear being "out of the loop" or "out of sight, out of mind" because the networks *are* the loop and what is seen.

10

WHAT'S NEXT?

Heat creates energy; this is signified by the wind stirred up by the fire and issuing forth from it. This represents influence working from within outward. . . . In order to be capable of producing such an influence, one's words must have power, and this they can have only if they are based on something real, just as flame depends on its fuel.
—The I Ching, Book One, *Hexagram 37*

Working virtually is fast unfolding and changing our perception of the new economy. This path is a fast one, and what is possible today is but a shadow of what will be possible in the near future. This is the hope, the promise, and the unsettling reality. For those of us walking (or running) on this path, we can rest assured that we are and will continue to be learners, evolvers, change masters. Human resources, training, information sharing, leadership development, learning will continue to evolve with virtual possibilities. Our organizations continue to have the option to increasingly align cultures and structures with visions of networked, global entities.

And people will continue to be the key to transformation. Technology has and continues to make new ways of "thinking" possible. Leadership is increasingly a function of connecting networks of interdependent systems, people, visions, focused attention, purpose. It includes leading through influence, introduction, and facilitation of sustainable virtual relationships—across silos and tribes, across boundaries and walls, beyond traditional organizational beginnings and endings.

Our collective "corporate" beliefs are open to exploration, question, expansion, perhaps even dissolution. For example, does digital information have to lose richness in translation? Are electronic relationships of a lower quality? Is emotional bandwidth impossible without physical presence? Are business systems autonomous and independent from one another, or are they porous membranes, open systems networked together more than we even knew?

Organizations are at the edge of a new frontier of not only embracing the technical capabilities and individual technical competencies, but also of redefining "productivity" and "work." All organizations and individuals can make significant gains in their virtual competencies. Organizations and individuals will self-determine how competent they will be, and what else is or is not possible.

Until the definitions of "productivity" and "work" can be deeply expanded, however, most organizations will stay in struggle to some degree, making it a challenge to step into truly sustainable virtual work.

This may seem a dire prediction after such a hopefully written book; *it is not.* It is a challenge to take the bold, brave step as leaders to examine the possibilities, to live into the future. This author believes that organizations have a better chance at creating sustainable futures for the organizations and the people working in them if leaders begin to redefine productivity. In fact, I see virtual work as a wonderful window of opportunity for organizations and leaders to really look at their performance management practices and possibly *truly* move to a management-by-results focus. The definition of productivity itself broadens.

Wouldn't it be nice if conversation and reflection were actually built in as a viable productivity measurement? Forums like online communities are increasingly important learning sources for many; why not reward such deep thinking in the organization itself? Why couldn't productivity include deep thinking and interdependence with each other, resulting in more informed action that produces value-added outcomes congruent to the mission and for the customer? Because of the virtual environment, I see teams actually valuing and getting rewarded for building social relationships within and among teams, and using networks as a primary vehicle of "work." Won't it be nice to see *that* as a productivity measure?

Yes, in an ideal world, but who has the time? It is true that we, thanks (and no thanks) to technology, are now expecting and expected to move at top speed. At the same time, I also find that conversations still need to and do happen, even if done while running down the hall. I keep circling back to the value of balancing movement (speed may be an unfortunate accepted reality in corporations today) with reflection. With no reflection, speed can result in quickly getting to the wrong destination. Reflection with no movement does result in expectations not met and, eventually, bankruptcy.

Organizations actually have an advantage in achieving bottom line results through true "community" and networks because they have the focusing alignment of mission as a reason—the umbrella purpose, if you will—for people collaborating. Mission, shared vision, strategic priorities, stakeholders' expectations, and customers—all focus the organizational members. I find the challenge in organizational members (employees) not so much their individual commitments to community (whether they call it "community" or not), so much as in connecting all the subcommunities (tribes and silos) back to the organizational charter. Here is where networked organizations and virtuality can paradoxically help break away from such limiting boundaries. Networked organizations that communicate shared meaning provide a virtual common ground upon which all stand together, connected by shared purpose and technology.

Organizations can begin their virtual journey simply with such tools as group scheduling and conference calls. Fully empowered virtual organizations, leaders, and workers, however, are more than a collection of tools. Virtual organizations commit to systemic structures and cultures that support collaboration and community fully. Organizations exist to *do something,* usually to provide products and/or services to some customer(s). In global, networked, virtual organizations, collaboration and community building are *vehicles for work.*

In doing research for his book,[31] Bill Jensen discovered that Generation Y workers blur the boundary between face-to-face and online relationships fairly easily. This is the first generation that "grew up" online, so they have a comfort in the environment that is ingrained.

---

[31]Bill Jensen, *Simplicity: The New Competitive Advantage in a World of More, Better, Faster* (Perseus Press, February 2000).

They *expect* work to be virtual and relational, and they see no disconnect between the two. In fact, if organizations focus on creating environments that are trustworthy and collaborative and provide tools that work simply, the table is set for virtual team members to think about their relationships and what they are doing together, instead of being distracted by trying to figure out how something works, or how to stay visible on the career path, or whether this virtual adventure is a good risk.

Free people to focus on forming team relationships that are focused on performance, and they will! The organization should focus on the culture, the systems, the environment, the tools, and the support. As one member of a recent online dialogue group on virtual teams stated, "Get that right, and you can put a team on a bus with Dixie cups and string for communication devices and they'll probably soar!"

Attracting and retaining the best talent is critical. This book has stated many reasons why virtual work makes sense. If attracting and retaining the youngest generation of professionals is more likely if the organization has the right virtual tools, solutions, and environment, then senior leadership has yet another compelling reason to move forward aggressively beyond an occasional telecommuter and group calendars.

If an organization is in integrity, just as a person, then trust gets built with its members. How practical, simple, elegant, and difficult this is for some people, and for some organizations. And yet, how wonderful when found. One of my overriding values is to find ways to make it easy for people—and organizations—to succeed, to meet expectations and, therefore, to be in integrity. In helping teams do this, I see incredible transformation of dysfunctional work groups to mission-aligned teams.

When team leaders, organizations, and members value this, how much can change? This applies in both virtual and co-located environments. What is advantageous in virtual environments is that everyone knows she or he needs to rely on communication and intentional context, commitments, and results. In co-located environments, I wonder if we sometimes rely too heavily on what is convenient—habit, nonverbal cues, proximity—and don't fully focus on the whole relationship. There are obviously differences between organization and member trust, and team member trust, but when I was researching for this

book and examining my own and client work over the]
really notice one recurring theme:

> *People enjoy being on teams and in communities where they feel connected, supported, and the work they do matters and makes a difference.*

In closing, a virtual colleague shared a story that I'd like to paraphrase. A group of us were discussing the questions of virtual trust and the sustainability of global work relationships. This gentleman told the story of his Scotland family's multi-generation lumber business. At least three generations back, lumber was bought in Scotland from lumberjacks in the western United States and transported by business people from multiple countries. All this contractual work was struck based on people's word—not even a handshake was involved over the ocean and many miles.

Relationships were built on trust, time, and results. Before there ever was a three-fold path, this family-owned business, along with several other businesses across nationalities, formed long-lasting, cohesive relationships (pathway one) that supported one another's longevity and profitability (pathway two). They sustained these relationships by producing successful outcomes (pathway three). This story is proof that, while virtual work requires a significant paradigm shift, it really is nothing new. There is a tradition of virtual relationships that precedes the terminology and the technology.

If a three-plus generation family business can function virtually 40 years ago without the tools, the technology, or the handshake, how much more is possible today?

APPENDIX

ADDITIONAL RESOURCES

SAMPLE TOOL A

ORGANIZATION DEVELOPMENT VIRTUAL READINESS INTERVIEW AND FOCUS GROUP INTERVIEW QUESTIONS

Virtual Work Goals, Objectives, and Parameters

- How do people in various parts of the organization define virtual work? Virtual teams? For example, *part-time or full-time telecommuter, road warrior, remote office*

- How do people see virtual work supporting the organizational mission?

- How many people are interested in participating in virtual teams? How many managers?

- What are the drivers and the intention behind a move to virtual work? For example, *competition, recruiting/retention, balance*

- What should be the short- and long-range objectives for your virtual environment? For example, *increased productivity, reduced real estate, increased speed to market*

Strategic Priorities, Values, and Leadership

- Review organizational culture, values, and guiding principles and see how virtual work supports or contradicts.

- How are strategy and other critical communications communicated within the corporation? For example, *newsletter, department meetings, paycheck stuffers, web casts*

- How does learning get defined and done around here? For example, *classroom, online learning, self-paced computer-based modules, on the job*

- What is the leadership style in this organization? For example, *collaborative, authoritarian, consensus, situational*

- What is the overall communication style? Meeting style? For example, *casual, formal, written, oral*

- How does the company value family and work life balance? For example, *Are there flex schedule options? On-site day care? Telecommuting initiative?*

Communication and Overall Organization Effectiveness

- What organizational "habits" will impact successful virtual work? For example, *common last-minute "huddle" meetings, posting information updates to internal web sites, celebrating birthdays in break rooms*

- How do divisions, departments, and geographically disbursed areas communicate and report?

- Are there any cultural leaders or heroes? What makes them so? (lone rangers, crisis managers, coaches, etc.)

- What are considered "perks" around here? For example, *larger office with a door, personal administrative assistant, title*

Workflow

- How prepared is information technology to support a networked organization? A knowledge management system?

- How congruent are workflows with virtual work? For example, *primarily paperless handoffs, electronic signatures*

Policies

- Are there any corporate policies that appear to contradict a virtual environment? That will be impacted by virtual teams?

- What is essential to include in a virtual work policy?

Human Resource Management

- What are your policies/systems regarding performance management? How is performance measured? For example, *Individual performance? Group performance? Both? Incentives?*

- How do rewards and consequences apply?

- How does this organization train and develop people? For example, *hire experienced only, no/little training; computer and Internet-based; classroom; on the job; coaching and mentoring*

Risk Management

- What areas of the company are the most resistant to change or would be the biggest barriers to telecommuting? Why?

- What are the organization's liability issues and concerns in a virtual work environment?

Support

- What are the most compelling reasons to implement virtual work?

- What will help it succeed here?

- Are you interested in virtual work yourself? Why or why not?

SAMPLE TOOL B

VIRTUAL TEAM MEMBER READINESS SELF-ASSESSMENT

	Disagree	Agree	Strongly Agree
Organization Culture and Home Site Factors			
I am confident that I can influence my career path as a virtual worker.			
I avoid distractions in my environment and am able to stay focused on tasks.			
I have a designated workspace that is separate from my family and home activities and has adequate workspace.			
My designated workspace has adequate heating/cooling and lighting to ensure a safe work environment.			
I can effectively access the Inter/intranet from my remote office.			
My household members know to respect my work boundaries while I am working.			
With reasonable accommodations, I have the tools and resources I need to work remotely.			

	Disagree	Agree	Strongly Agree
I can arrange for dependent care.			
I could work from home without causing any significant disruption to my colleagues and clients.			
I know how to get what I need done in the organization.			
I can reasonably accommodate a home-based work schedule with essential face-to-face client/collegial meetings.			
I know whom I need to communicate with, how often, and in what ways in order to ensure quality work results.			
My manager has the skills needed to manage my performance from a distance and for results.			
Competencies and Experience Factors			
I can perform to standard without constant supervision.			
I can identify the resources I need to meet performance expectations.			
I am comfortable not always including others in many job-related decisions.			
I am confident making independent decisions.			
I am currently capable of performing over half my job functions without direct supervision.			
I know when to include my manager or others in a decision or work issue.			
I currently meet my manager and team's expectations on this job.			

	Disagree	Agree	Strongly Agree
My performance appraisal ratings are average and above.			
I have been performing this job long enough to do so without frequent coaching.			
I am able to utilize technology effectively to complete work tasks and facilitate information flow.			
I can do basic troubleshooting when I face technical difficulties.			
I know how to organize my work effectively in order to meet performance expectations, including organizing between remote and on-site workstations.			
I can effectively plan for tasks and projects.			
I am increasingly effective at work due to my evaluation of past performance.			
I initiate communication regarding tasks and projects that contribute to increased team output.			
My manager is familiar with my performance and trusts me to do my job.			
I am generally considered a highly organized person.			
I have the kind of manager who can manage by objectives and doesn't need to constantly oversee my work.			
My supervisor and I have a good relationship based on mutual trust.			

	Disagree	Agree	Strongly Agree
I have been at the company for some time, and I am fully familiar with its culture, policies, and procedures.			
I consider myself to be highly technology- and software-literate.			
When a problem arises with a colleague or customer, I can confront it honestly and with kindness and a view toward positive resolution.			
Characteristics and Qualities			
I am self-disciplined.			
I know how to start and stop work.			
I am comfortable with shifting resources and expectations during a project.			
I am reliable and meet deadlines with little supervision.			
I am a self-starter.			
I can effectively ask for input and feedback.			
I am resourceful and innovative in completing job tasks and overcoming barriers.			
I like working independently.			
I like working in a team environment.			
I like the idea of working in a virtual environment.			
I am able to anticipate and plan for project issues and delays.			
I am able to clearly and consistently evaluate my own performance.			

	Disagree	Agree	Strongly Agree
I initiate projects and tasks without direct supervision.			
I have a clear idea and systems in place about how and when to inform those I work with or for.			
I enjoy working alone; in fact, I prefer it.			
I find it relatively easy to get persistent people off the telephone or my doorstep.			
I feel I can effectively separate my work and home lives and can "switch off" when the workday ends.			
I am committed to helping my team to succeed.			

SAMPLE TOOL C

VIRTUAL TEAM MANAGER READINESS SELF-ASSESSMENT CHECKLIST

	Disagree	Agree	Strongly Agree
I am able to schedule and utilize my resources (people, equipment, etc.) effectively to create a product/service without having to oversee the project at all times.			
I am familiar with my team members' performance and trust them to do the job.			
My team supports virtual work.			
I support virtual work.			
I have the skills needed to manage my team's performance from a distance and for results.			
Each virtual employee and I know how to organize his/her work effectively in order to meet performance expectations, including organizing between virtual and on-site workstations.			

	Disagree	Agree	Strongly Agree
Systems are in place about how and when virtual workers need to inform those they work with and for.			
The job descriptions I manage are partially or fully "virtually workable."			
I manage my in-house team well, but would like assistance in developing my distance management skills.			
I have clear communication systems and feedback mechanisms in place.			
I am familiar with each of my team members' performance.			
I trust my team members.			
I coach my team members to develop to their fullest potential.			
I have contingency plans for delays and other project interruptions or changes.			
I delegate responsibility and authority effectively.			
I provide clear direction to my team, enabling them to work without constant supervision.			
I manage for results, and can clearly communicate my performance expectations.			
I can scout for career opportunities for my remote team members and provide virtual access to those opportunities.			

SAMPLE TOOL D

SAMPLE TEAM DEVELOPMENT PROCESS CHECKLIST

Provided here is a complete checklist of areas and starter questions to consider in building a team development planning agenda. It may be used as a complete agenda to be discussed with a newly formed team, or it may be modified. While lengthy, this checklist is an attempt to anticipate all areas of team functioning and effectiveness that are impacted in a virtual environment.

I. Getting Acquainted
   a. Career aspirations?
   b. Background?
      i. Hobbies and interests?
      ii. Experience, expertise, education?
   c. Strengths and challenge areas?
   d. Experience with virtual work?
   e. Motivations?

II. Team Charter, Vision, Values
   a. What is our charter?
   b. What are the organization and stakeholders' expectations?
   c. What are our expectations?
   d. What atmosphere do we want to create?
      i. Create a project/team symbol to unite team across distances
      ii. Organize reward, recognition systems to support the team
      iii. Decide level of formality, familiarity, structure, and flow
      iv. Recreate virtual celebration rituals

III. Team/Project Planning
  a. Project goals?
  b. Have or can get all needed resources?
  c. Deadlines, milestones, and deliverables?
      i. How "real" are they?
      ii. What's negotiable and what's firm?
      iii. What does accomplishment/success look like?
      iv. What are acceptable performance standards?
  d. Individual and team project roles, responsibilities, and authority?
      i. Each team member's role and responsibilities for each deadline, deliverable?
      ii. Where does individual authority to decide or act begin and end?
      iii. Who will take or share responsibility for virtual team roles?
  e. How will implicit knowledge and learning be made explicit?
  f. How will we replace or re-create learning by observation?
  g. How will we coach one another?
  h. How will we embed learning together?
  i. How will we measure and evaluate ourselves?
  j. Do we have any influence over how we compensate ourselves individually and as a team?
  k. What are our ground rules, working agreements, and commitments to the team?
  l. What are our operating procedures and systems?
      i. Do they support our communication needs?
      ii. Do they support our project charter?
      iii. Are they simple and easy to use?
IV. Getting Acquainted II
  a. Comfort with virtual tools?
  b. Input needed to feel included?
  c. What needed to feel empowered?
  d. What does support look like?
  e. How prefer to be managed? Followed?
  f. Hot buttons?

    g. Communication media and feedback preferences?
       i. Contact information
          1. Telephone, wireless phone, voicemail, fax, email, pager
          2. Technological limitations (software, document attachment size, etc.)
       ii. Preferred order of contact media
    h. Who has what project roles and responsibilities?
V. Team Process Planning
    a. What kinds of problems merit a group effort?
       i. Affects all and not resolvable with current systems or structures
       ii. New and uncharted problems
       iii. Old and stubborn problems
       iv. Little consensus
    b. Who needs to participate in what decisions, actions, and commitments made on behalf of the team?
       i. What authority levels need further definition?
    c. How will we meet?
       i. When and why synchronous?
          1. In person?
          2. Audio, videoconference?
          3. Chat?
       ii. When asynchronous?
          1. Listserves and email?
          2. Voicemail?
          3. Recorded meetings?
          4. How use threads?
    d. How will we use groupware and other tools?
       i. How will documents be shared and modified?
          1. Same time together?
          2. Same time separately in parallel?
          3. Sequentially?
          4. When and how are modifications draft only? Adopted?
       ii. How will information be shared?
       iii. What security measures need to be taken?

        iv. How well are our protocols and infrastructure supported by the organization? And the reverse?

VI. Communication Infrastructure

    a. What are our standards?

        i. Availability to one another (hours of availability, time zone, emergency availability)

        ii. Document usage (e.g., page and version numbers on documents)

        iii. Required meetings, attendance options (virtual or in person), group scheduling and notification of attendance protocols

    b. What will we use as anchors to verify shared agreement and understanding?

    c. What is our communication flow?

        i. Who needs to talk to whom about what through what medium?

        ii. How often and who else needs to be informed or involved?

        iii. What issues command full team attention and what is the medium?

        iv. How will knowledge be managed and shared?

            1. How much information sharing is enough? Too much?

            2. What's the preferred format? Protocols?

                a. Pushed?

                b. Pulled?

                c. Posted?

        v. Who is the first point of contact for what kinds of issues or questions?

        vi. What does help look like for this team?

            1. What is full support and participation?

            2. What is appropriate to ask for, offer, leave alone? And by whom?

VII. Membership and Maintenance

    a. Who has what role responsibilities?

        i. Media specialist

        ii. Process manager

        iii. Knowledge manager/protocol overseer

    b. How will we ensure "membership"?

c. How will we support, confront one another?

d. How will we agree to manage conflict, discomfort, and confusion?

e. Do we need a virtual water cooler?

f. Do we need electronic newsletters, team web site, electronic yearbooks?

Consult One Group Company
Profile and Personal Biography

Bringing spirit back to organizations and their people
www.consultonegroup.com

Trina Hoefling, founder of Consult One Group of Colorado, is an organizational psychologist, executive coach, and shadow consultant. Ms. Hoefling has more than 18 years experience in organization development, management consulting, coaching, and training. She has been involved in the design, development, and implementation of virtual work initiatives dating back to 1984. Her other primary consulting work includes organizational and team consulting, shadow consulting, individual coaching, and speaking engagements. She has presented internationally on many subjects, including virtual work, telecommuting, and virtual teaming. Trina holds two M.A. degrees in Industrial/Organizational Psychology and Communication.

Her expertise primarily involves the following areas:

- Executive and entrepreneurial coaching
- Executive team development and coaching
- Organizational alignment assessments and strategies
- Organization development and cultural change management
- Virtual and co-located team effectiveness assessment and development
- Shadow consulting

Trina works with the airline and ground transportation industries; telephony and technology; health care; government departments; retail; service; professional and consulting businesses; and nonprofit organizations. She has worked with frontline employees, supervisory and middle management, top management, owners, and executive boards.

Trina is increasingly being retained for individual professional and business coaching, as well as change management and human resources shadow consulting. Trina is "a consultant's consultant." Called shadow consulting, she works invisibly "behind the scenes" as a resource to consultants. She works with internal and external consultants and teams to identify core client issues, strategic approaches, appropriate interventions, and systemic implications of various approaches.

Trina is also an experienced public speaker and has presented nationally and internationally on virtual work and other subjects.

Consult One Group of Colorado is a company that helps organizations and their people to grow effectively. It is a full service management and organization development consulting firm which is dedicated to helping build spirit into every aspect of client organizations. Trina and her associates support sustainable and steady effectiveness for organizations and their people.

COG's philosophy is to identify and work the *right* issues, instead of forcing a packaged fit or throwing a Band-Aid on a symptom. They identify the "high leverage intervention" which can be much simpler, less expensive, and more subtle than the "symptom" might suggest.

For more information, contact Consult One Group at *www.consultonegroup.com* or Trina personally at *trinah@consultonegroup.com*.